Blue Jeans

Blue Jeans

The Art of the Ordinary

Daniel Miller and Sophie Woodward

UNIVERSITY OF CALIFORNIA PRESS

Berkeley · Los Angeles · London

University of California Press, one of the most distinguished university presses in the United States, enriches lives around the world by advancing scholarship in the humanities, social sciences, and natural sciences. Its activities are supported by the UC Press Foundation and by philanthropic contributions from individuals and institutions. For more information, visit www.ucpress.edu.

University of California Press
Berkeley and Los Angeles, California

University of California Press, Ltd.
London, England

Library of Congress Cataloging-in-Publication Data

Miller, Daniel, 1954–
  Blue jeans : the art of the ordinary / Daniel Miller and Sophie Woodward.
    p. cm.
  Includes bibliographical references.
  ISBN 978-0-520-27218-7 (cloth : alk. paper) — ISBN 978-0-520-27219-4 (pbk. : alk. paper) 1. Jeans (Clothing)—Social aspects. 2. Denim—Social aspects. 3. Clothing and dress. 4. Material culture. I. Woodward, Sophie. II. Title.
GT2085.M55 2011
391.4'76—dc23

2011036634

Manufactured in the United States of America

20 19 18 17 16 15 14 13 12 11
10 9 8 7 6 5 4 3 2 1

In keeping with a commitment to support environmentally responsible and sustainable printing practices, UC Press has printed this book on Rolland Enviro100, a 100% post-consumer fiber paper that is FSC certified, deinked, processed chlorine-free, and manufactured with renewable biogas energy. It is acid-free and EcoLogo certified.

Contents

Acknowledgments

As always in such work, our first acknowledgment has to be to our participants. We are always amazed, but also very grateful, when so many people agree to open their doors and give us time, especially when there can be little pretense that a topic such as denim would ever be of much direct benefit to them. There is something about the graciousness of ordinary people that a project such as this brings out, and it is always worth acknowledging. We are very grateful too for the help of Alesya Krit and Sabrina Miller, our two interns. Given our commitments to teaching and university administrative duties, we could not have done this research without a grant toward the transcribing of interviews from The British Academy (award number SG-49624), the only funding we had for this project. We would also like to thank Naomi Braithwaite, who helped collect background bibliographic information and collate our more quantitative information. An earlier version of chapter 7 appeared in *American Ethnologist* as "Anthropology in Blue Jeans."

Introduction

This book is intended to advance contemporary material culture studies. We draw on interviews and observations of how people select and wear blue jeans in our effort to create a theory of the ordinary and its place in social science.* This theory of the ordinary has major consequences for topics ranging from immigration to questions of identity, equality, and the routine. While such a claim might initially appear to be somewhat grandiose, our aim is to arrive at these theoretical contributions through the course of this book, building upon the collection and analysis of empirical observations. The inspiration behind this sequence lies in Claude Lévi-Strauss's exhortation to anthropologists to rethink the limits of their enterprise by considering the discipline to be a kind of philosophy by other means. This book may be read both by those who are simply interested in why people wear blue jeans and also by people with no interest in clothing, as the topic of jeans is used to create a contribution to the study of humanity more generally through our theory of the ordinary.

* In this volume the terms *blue jeans* and *denim* are generally synonymous, which accords with the usage of our informants, though on occasion we will refer to items other than jeans made from denim.

The intention is not at all to replicate philosophy itself. At least since the time of Bertrand Russell philosophy has come to recognize its affinity with mathematics in that both are modes in which an abstraction is understood as a relationship between other abstractions. Points are illustrated with material from the world of everyday life but utilized at this more abstract level. By contrast, this book starts from the world itself and has no desire to lose its attachment to everyday life through overly abstract generalization. Rather, a discipline such as anthropology acknowledges that it is the people we study who in their myths and religions but also in their everyday routines and actions may be creating an order in the world analogous to formal philosophy. Lévi-Strauss's contention can be extended to the enterprise of many other social sciences, and his sentiment finds support in writings from very different traditions, which acknowledge that the seemingly mundane and routine are clues to the profound. Yet even among those who seem sympathetic to this ideal, getting the balance right is difficult. The work of Judith Butler may be criticized for not basing theories of the mundane upon in-depth substantive research, while at the other end Erving Goffman is praised for the meticulous nature of his observations but others wish he would have gone further in his exploration of the philosophical implications of his analyses. Elsewhere, Miller has characterized this ambition for anthropology, a discipline that seems to retain the most extreme devotion to empirical studies, as in ethnography, which involves at least a year's engagement with some population. And yet anthropologists aspire, as part of the same project, to make generalizations and theory pertaining to humanity as a whole (Miller 2010, 6–11). The contrast is with middle-range academic work that narrowly delineates hypotheses that are tested through methods such as questionnaires or focus groups.

This was the ambition behind the project described in this volume. We start on the gentle slopes of ethnographic reporting, describing the people of three streets in North London through the way they relate to blue jeans. We then climb up to vantage points from which we can consider more analytical concepts derived from this ethnography, such as the meaning of the words *comfort* and *ordinary*. Finally we argue that these results have implications for our fundamental understanding of how societies reproduce, construct, and control themselves, the foundational building blocks of social science.

This approach does not employ hypotheses, in the sense that when we started this project we had no idea at all about which abstract or theoretical issues our material might eventually contribute to. The original question behind this research was a very simple one: why do so many people wear jeans? Woodward's (2007) previous ethnography of women's wardrobes in the United Kingdom highlighted the extent to which people wore jeans as an everyday item of clothing. Yet despite a flourishing discipline of clothing studies there was no literature explicitly on denim or jeans that offered any account as to why jeans had become so dominant. As we started developing our research in the area, we rapidly became aware that the topic was far too big for just the two of us, given the global spread of jeans. On that basis, we started what we called the Global Denim Project, to encourage other researchers to exchange ideas and data on this topic.

By the time we reached the stage of carrying out the ethnography that forms the basis for this book, we had formulated some initial ideas around notions of anxiety and the role denim might have in alleviating it. But, as often happens in ethnography, this almost entirely faded from view because it wasn't the perspective that seemed to fit best with the observations we started making in these streets. While it was always obvious that denim could be described as ordinary, the suggestion that this might be the key to our findings didn't occur to us in anything like the guise in which it appears in this book until around six months into our fieldwork. Indeed, we were almost disappointed that there was nothing more shocking and unusual in our findings. Initially the word *ordinary* seemed so banal, more a taken-for-granted background than a pretender to the crown of accomplished research. For the same reason, arriving at a sense of the profundity and importance of ordinariness took even longer.

Yet in retrospect we had made several decisions that made this orientation that much more likely. The most obvious is our choice of topic: denim. Originally we didn't much use the word *ordinary,* not even in our discussions, instead emphasizing slightly more academic words such as *ubiquitous* or *mundane.* But at that point we were not sure what aspects of blue jeans would become prominent. Depending upon the ethnographic material, we might well have ended up emphasizing designer jeans, the diversity of jeans, issues of style, or aspects of denim that were anything but ordinary. We might have seen them as evidence for oppressive conformity, commercial guile, or global Americanization. The original ground for selecting denim as a topic was simply an observation about clothing and fashion studies more generally: that the less people wore particular genres of clothing, the more those were the clothes that seemed to be written about. There were floods of articles about designers and catwalks based on garments you would never see other than in the media, while very little was written about denim itself, although it clearly dominates what most people wear most of the time.

In order to gain some sense of the scale and scope of denim, we started to estimate the proportion of jeans that people were wearing in whichever country we visited, standing on a street corner and taking notes on the first hundred people to walk by. We found that in most countries outside of South Asia and China, perhaps half the population was wearing denim on any given day. Commercial research suggested that the global average is for people to wear jeans 3.5 days a week (Global Lifestyle Monitor 2008), with the highest frequency being in Germany, where jeans are worn 5.2 days of the week (and ownership is on average 8.6 pairs per person). Globally, more than six out of ten consumers (62 percent) say they love or enjoy wearing denim, with the highest responses coming in Brazil (72 percent). By contrast, in India a mere 27 percent state that they love wearing jeans. According to a recent global survey (Synovate 2008), 31 percent of people in the countries surveyed, ranging from the United States and Russia to Korea and South Africa, own three or four pairs of jeans; 29 percent own between five and ten pairs of jeans. In Brazil, 14 percent of respondents own ten or more pairs of jeans, and 40 percent own five to ten pairs. The number of people who do not own jeans is relatively low, with, for example, 13 percent of Russians not owning jeans, though the figure for Malaysia reaches 29 percent. We suspect that such commercial research neglects the vast populations of rural China and South Asia, but other than that, the term *global* seems fully justified.

These statistics give foundation to our emerging ideas of the global spread of blue jeans, yet in themselves they are not sufficient to afford any kind of explanation. We initiated our own project with a publication called "A Manifesto for the Study of Denim" (Miller and Woodward 2007) and followed this by setting up the Global Denim Project, which now has its own website (www.ucl.ac.uk/global-denim-project) and several associated publications (Miller and Woodward 2011; Woodward and Miller 2011). This project was intended to use denim both to address issues such as globalization and local difference and to think about how social science could examine specific local cultural forms and at the same time deal with items that seemed ubiquitous across the world. From the research of the scholars who joined with us in this project have emerged some tentative answers to the larger question of why people wear blue jeans.

Other publications have covered ground different from that explored in this volume, such as the history of denim, its production, and sales (e.g., Chakravarti 2011; Comstock 2011; Pinheiro 2011; Wilkinson-Weber 2011). By contrast, the present volume focuses on our ethnography of possessing and wearing jeans. Still, the central question behind all these research projects remains: why jeans? For many this would appear to lead naturally to the route of historically tracing the origins of jeans. Indeed, much of the literature on denim and jeans falls within the disciplinary rubric of history (and often popular history). This includes the histories of both indigo and the textile denim. The former traces the origins of the blue color of denim to the mere happenstance that the plant-based dye indigo fixes its color to cloth without needing a mordant, the substance that is used to fix other dyes to cloth. This is what made indigo one of the key world crops from ancient times to colonial times (Balfour-Paul 1998; Taussig 2008). There is an equally well established history of cotton, which alongside indigo would give us an understanding of many aspects of human history, from the global evolution of political economy down to periodic fashions and styles in almost any part of the world (Riello and Parthasarathi 2009; South Carolina Cotton Museum 2007). There is also now a well-established historical perspective on blue jeans more generally, from the patenting of the rivets by Levi Strauss to the icons James Dean, Marilyn Monroe, and John Wayne (see Sullivan 2006).

There is a limit, however, to the degree to which historical research can account for a contemporary phenomenon. There are many products and activities that have deep historical trajectories, from ceramics to poultry keeping, though this does not ensure that they will have the same ubiquity today that they possessed in precapitalist or preindustrial periods. There were times when indigo was not particularly prominent, while blue jeans themselves were developed only in the late nineteenth century. So there had to be other factors to account for the rise of blue jeans as a contemporary global form. It has become common in social science to explain global commodities by asserting that capitalism persuades people to adopt whatever contributes to the maximization of profit. But from a commercial perspective, although firms make money from jeans, they would make much more money from clothes that went out of fashion each year, that were worn less often, and whose typical examples changed a bit more over time. Obviously companies make money from jeans, but there is no evidence that capitalism as an economic system favors jeans; quite the contrary. So the obvious reasons for wearing jeans—their history or their commercial value—are insufficient if we want to account for the growing domination of denim today.

Our Global Denim Project was designed to rethink much of this, challenging some of the history (Comstock 2011), but most of all confronting this object from a more ethnographic perspective that recognized that denim is not simply a form of global homogenization or conformity. Each region, from Brazil (Mizrahi 2011), China (McDonald 2011), and England (Woodward 2011) to Germany (Ege 2011), India (Miller 2011), and Italy (Sassatelli 2011), has a local configuration that explains why people do or do not wear jeans. Similarly, there are more specific issues of production (Chakravarti 2011), styling (Keet 2011), marketing (Wilkinson-Weber 2011), retailing (Pinheiro 2011), and even recycling (Olesen 2011). The aim of the Global Denim Project was both to acknowledge all these specific studies and to transcend them through the consideration of more general issues. There were other properties that seemed unique to denim as well. For example, it has an ability, after being worn extensively, to soften—a process that was then copied in the manufacture of jeans through various processes of "distressing" (Miller 2009a). Mostly the material properties of denim are analyzed within the literature of textile technology and color chemistry by considering the properties of fabric itself (Tarhan and Sarsiisik 2009; Chowdhary 2002), among other things. However, the understanding of the material's properties rarely occurs in conjunction with an understanding of their social implications. For example, considering the properties of indigo as a dye and the ways in which denim is woven that lead to it softening or fading can help us understand how denim becomes personalized to the shape of the wearer.

It was not a coincidence, we concluded, that people not only regard jeans as having a greater capacity than other garments to become intimate and personal as they soften and mold to a particular body but also see wearing this global garment as the best means to present themselves as citizens of the world. Living with an increasing consciousness of the sheer scale of an often alienating world, people want to lay claim to being part of that world, but fear that in doing so they will lose their sense of individuality and specificity. So to have one garment that is simultaneously extremely personal and extremely ubiquitous can be important in its own right. Merely wearing jeans can be a way of resolving this contradiction, of becoming more personal and more global at the same time. Curiously, we found that jeans seem to echo the academic ideal we started with: to bring the generalities of philosophy and the specificity and diversity of the everyday back into communion with each other. We had found a way to bring both Levi Strauss and Lévi-Strauss into our equation.

The Global Denim Project was very successful as a kind of "open-source" project linking disparate research, both highly specific studies and ideas about jeans as a global presence (Miller and Woodward 2011; Woodward and Miller 2011). It is by no means complete as a project, and we hope there will be many more of these studies over the next few years, addressing issues both parochial and global. But we also had reasons for considering denim nearer to home. Part of the grounds for choosing this topic came from our own respective research in England. Woodward had written a PhD thesis (subsequently published) on how women chose what to wear from their wardrobes, and came to the conclusion that denim represented a kind of default wardrobe mode that was central to understanding clothing choice as a whole (Woodward 2007). Through an in-depth ethnography, jeans emerged as the item that, for many women, bridges habitual clothing (items women "know" they can always wear) and the nonhabitual (items that require a self-conscious engagement). This is achieved through denim's perceived high combinational potential, something to be either dressed down or dressed up. Miller, working with Clarke, had argued on the basis of research on clothes shopping that theories of fashion ought to start not from the designer but from the sense of anxiety that so many people seem to feel when making choices about what to wear (Clarke and Miller 2002). So as well as going broader through the Global Denim Project, we had the ambition to go deeper by devoting an entire ethnographic study to jeans in a single location. This was the reasoning behind our research in London.

THE ARGUMENT

This book started with our feet quite literally on the ground, constantly walking up and down three North London streets. The structure of the book mirrors the progression to theory we noted as our opening ambition. The first section of the book engages specifically with the ethnography of jeans wearing. A key part of each interview was to ask people about their life history through jeans, and also about their current jeans-wearing practices. True to the ethnographic tradition, this was situated in their lives more widely, in terms of their work, relationships, and issues such as how they felt about their body. The next three chapters follow from the mode of investigation and examine denim as clothing and the changing relationship people have to their jeans, as well as how this may have changed in the course of their lives. This includes a focus upon the links between jeans, generations, and life stages. We then widen this out to the household and the role that denim plays in mediating and constructing people's relationships, whether between members of a couple, between friends, or between parents and sons or daughters. This section finishes with a final chapter on people's purchase of jeans and how they use jeans to order and organize different aspects of their lives. It also discusses the sometimes fraught relationship to fashion, which in turn exposes a quite complex field in which jeans may simultaneously be always in fashion, part of the fashion of a particular period, and anti-fashion.

The next section focuses upon denim and the ordinary as we start to theorize the single most common reason people gave for choosing denim, which was "being comfortable." By looking more deeply at the semantics and usage of the word *comfort* we will see how it manages to bring together many key issues of modern life. From the perspective of comfort we move to a consideration of why, contrary to the general assumption that most people are trying to escape ordinariness and become in various ways extraordinary, our data reveal the opposite trajectory: that people are trying to become less marked and struggling to be regarded as entirely ordinary. We then needed to understand why people should wish to cultivate the art of being ordinary. We start with a group within this study for whom the explanation is easier to grasp, focusing one chapter on the immigrant populations represented in these streets. Having clarified some of the underlying imperatives, we are then ready to reach up to a more philosophical encounter with the role of the ordinary in understanding humanity more generally. This results in a section on the consequences of becoming ordinary, and why in the twenty-first century ordinariness may have reached an unprecedented significance in the self-determination of people in society.

At this point we leave aside these ethnographic findings to look at long-term trajectories and debates in social science more generally, especially anthropology and sociology. We will find there are many academic trajectories that lead to a consideration of the ordinary, with varied implications and consequences. Our task then becomes to try to find a meeting point between a concept of the ordinary derived from moving upward from our grounded research on denim and that coming down from theory in social science. In chapter 7 we argue that denim poses a challenge to the way anthropology has understood not only what society is but also how society reproduces itself over time. More specifically, we address how a focus on the ordinary challenges the principle of the normative as the foundation of anthropology. In our final chapter, we turn more to sociology: the gradual appreciation of the ordinary as a proper topic of study and how this has led to a focus on practical consciousness and routines that opens the door to the kind of material culture study represented by this book.

THE SETTING

Apart from the selection of blue jeans as a topic, the other key decision that led to this emphasis upon the ordinary was our choice of fieldwork location (though again this was not intentional). Location had been, from our point of view, largely a logistical issue. We lived in two very different parts of London and needed a place that was equally convenient in terms of transport. We also wanted to avoid extremes of wealth and poverty. Having calculated the approximate area, we found that a group of three connected streets seemed convenient. As it happens, they represented a rather homogeneous housing sector, while Miller in his previous London ethnographies (1998, 2008) had deliberately aimed for more mixed housing types.

Now, looking back after two years, it is hard to contemplate these streets other than through the lens of the almost extraordinarily ordinary. Apart from a small apartment complex on one corner and a shop on another corner, these are three streets of similar terraced properties without a single semidetached house. There is no pub, church, or any other intruding presence. The houses range from those that have been relatively gentrified to those that are more neglected, with paint peeling off the windows and the front yard run amok. Many have had their front yards wholly or partially paved to facilitate parking on the property, but the majority have some sort of garden, and these are mainly well tended. In summer, there is an abundance of roses and the typical British annuals such as petunias and lobelias, along with the standard perennials such as camellias and azaleas. Most have hedges, but these are generally quite low, so few houses are obscured from the public gaze.

These are "proper" streets in that one can see from one end to the other and there are almost always people in view. Children play in relatively safe public areas, since this is an enclave space that leads to nowhere in particular. There are no "rat runs," streets used by drivers to avoid

congestion or traffic lights; there are no free public parking spaces anywhere. One of the most common sights is that of beginning drivers with
their instructors; it seems the ideal place for a quiet introduction to mo-
toring. Most of the houses have small double-door porches where shoes
and Wellingtons can be kept. Some of the houses are pebble-dashed.
People seem to nod to each other and sometimes greet each other in
public, but it is less common to see long conversations between neighbors on the street itself.

Toward the end of our fieldwork we started to refer to this area as
a "silent community." The first clue to this designation came during the
summer, with an observation about canna lilies in front gardens. These
flowers seem rather more common in this neighborhood than one might
expect of English front yards and are not randomly distributed but seem
to cluster around groups of houses in particular areas. We then carried
out a more systematic survey of the external appearance of these houses
and noted that other items such as the distribution of burglar alarms
are clearly not random, but seem to cluster in much the same way. We
came to feel that this kind of contagion effect is quite possibly typical of
contemporary residential areas. It is not that people talk much to neighbors. As they themselves noted to us, communication is usually kept to
a friendly but superficial level of greeting. But, without saying anything,
they still keep at least one eye open to the behavior of their neighbors,
and if their neighbors are seen to do something, whether it is paving over
the front lawn or installing a porch, this has some impact upon whether
they are likely to do something similar. Keeping up with the Joneses
seems to be not a matter of status rivalry, as is usually assumed, but
more a respect for good ideas and being neighborly by retaining simi-
larity (compare McCracken 1989).

This was made explicit during a conversation with one of our participants, who said, "I think there is this unspoken community spirit;
people aren't really talking to each other, but they will notice what
everybody else is doing and thinking." So a silent community is one in
which people are expected to recognize and greet those who live in the
same area, but not to actually know them. This keeping an eye to the
street helps make the area feel relatively safe and secure. A surprising
number of households have no doorbells, and hardly anyone has entry
phones. Most front doors are set with panels of fake stained glass. There
are few explicit signs of identity: while we saw an occasional house
with an English flag, even fewer feature religious symbols, which, if
present, are of Islam or Hinduism. The only evident signs of its resolute

domesticity are a few front porch or front window signs with jokes about the dominance of women, for example, "This is a man's castle until a woman comes home."

Although one can find garden gnomes and even heraldic beasts, the streets seem so unremittingly removed from any sign of real wealth that there is no sense that such things would be regarded as vulgar. *Vulgar* implies differentiation or aspiration, but anyone who is looking to live in an area with even a smidgen of cool would move away from here as quickly as possible. This is mirrored in the living arrangements, as only 3 percent of participants were living in house shares with friends, an unusually low number for London. In contrast, 80 percent of participants were living with family (and of those, only 4 percent were living with just their partner). There is still a range of ages among the people living in the street, from those in their late teens through those in their eighties. The largest number of people we interviewed (28 percent) were in the age bracket forty to forty-nine, closely followed by the 25 percent of those between sixteen and twenty (only 19 percent of interviewees were over fifty). These are of course the statistics of those who were willing to be interviewed, rather than the entire population of these three streets. This is mirrored in the gender spread of participants: 64 percent of those interviewed were women, as they tended to be more willing participants.

Many of the younger people we interviewed were still living with their parents, and we had the feeling that even teenagers wouldn't bother being rowdy here, since there is no one around worth impressing with transgressive posturing. Instead, people settle into their interior spaces, which are much more diverse than the facades. We found both aesthetic minimalism, with barely any personal effects or decoration, and the minimalism of poverty, but mostly we saw both resolute respectability and relaxed disorder. The front rooms are often dominated by always-on large flat-screen TVs. The sense of ordinariness that this speaks to may have some young adults screaming with boredom as they wait to leave, but it probably has attracted immigrant families who feel this is an ideal, safe, secure place in which to put down roots alongside those indigenous families that have been living here for a long time (and who, in response to these newcomers, sport English flags in the front yard).

We started by delivering flyers about our project to the houses on all three streets and followed this up by knocking on doors and asking to come and discuss jeans at some more convenient time. We mainly worked over the summers of 2007 and 2008. People seemed friendlier during the summer, and frankly it was a much happier season for us to be left standing out in the road when they weren't. Many refused, while others wanted us to interview them immediately. Some required several visits, especially men, who had less affinity for discussing clothing than women. Ultimately a bit less than half of those we wanted to participate agreed to do so. This was a smaller proportion than in Miller's work in South London (2008), but then denim was less appealing as a topic than his previous topic, loss. Most of the interviews were done together, though some were done by just one or the other of us. We were fortunate also in having two interns as part of this project: in the first year Alesya Krit, who subsequently became a PhD student at the Department of Anthropology, University College London, and in the second year Sabrina Miller, Danny's niece, who was studying anthropology in California.

Ultimately there were sixty-seven individuals whom we count as informants/participants. Of these, 58 percent were born in the United Kingdom, although only 42 percent are white British, as many of the parents of those born in the United Kingdom were originally immigrants. Thirty-four percent were born in London, and around half of these were originally local. Just over a quarter of the participants come from families of South Asian origin, but this does not represent any sort of homogeneity, since their origins range from Indians arrived via East Africa to Pakistanis, Punjabis, and Bangladeshis, including Hindus, Muslims, and Sikhs. The rest are widely distributed in origin, including a few from Eastern Europe and West Africa, and then one or two each from a wide range of sites such as South America, the Caribbean, Hong Kong, Somalia, and Cyprus. This means nearly two-thirds are either first- or second-generation immigrants, though many of our actual participants, for example, from these South Asian families, were themselves born in Britain. Those on the street therefore range from the resolutely local (born on the street itself) to those who see this as a long-term residence suited to their immigrant status. In addition, there are some passing migrants, such as young Australians stopping here on their travels around Europe.

We always started with a standard questionnaire of around ten minutes, which allowed us to access personal details (such as age, gender, and place of birth) and data on their jeans, such as how many items they had. We found a questionnaire useful mainly because it served to put people at ease and provided some initial information that could be used to guide further discussion. We then proceeded to a kind of life history through jeans. This proved successful in getting most people to talk, and moreover was a crucial means for understanding how people's relationship with their clothing had developed. To try to give a more ethnographic complexion to the research, we worked hard to include several people from the same household in as many cases as possible. This was helped by our finding that there could be several houses belonging to relatives on our three target streets. In such cases it was often easy for us to find reasons to return, or at least have a chat in the street, so our sense of participants wasn't necessarily restricted to a single interview. In many cases, however, participation did mean only a single interview, although as this took place within the home, it still offered many insights beyond the interview itself (Hockey 2002), which we garnered from conversations around the formal interview, looking at the decor of the house, and meeting other family members who were present. The more ethnographic sense comes from the contextualization provided not just by our sense of the home interior and family life but also by virtue of being present and walking along the streets daily for the majority of two summers, which helped us gain a strong sense of place. This means we also came across our participants walking around on the street, and we became to them a relatively familiar presence, so we could expect to stop and chat with them as we passed by.

The project included families who have lived their entire life on these streets or close by. They describe how the housing was originally a local council development constructed at the end of World War II. They retain a nostalgia for what they see as the greater friendliness of the area at that time, with nearby plots used for gardening and a sense of neighborhood. Sometimes this decline in neighborhood is associated with the increase in immigrant families, but others seem reasonably sanguine about the growing cosmopolitanism or make it a point to say something positive about immigrant families. There is little evidence of this lost neighborhood in the present silent community. The only event anyone could recall (and quite a few did) was the public celebration of the queen's jubilee. The council agreed to shut off both ends of the area to prevent traffic, and there were bouncy castles and cupcakes for this memorable day.

Today the area retains its origins in state housing, and our participants included those still renting from the local council or from housing associations. But there has been a clear increase in private renting and private purchase. One part of the area certainly has a more South Asian emphasis: more of the doors were opened by people who couldn't speak

English. If people know each other at all, it is almost always through children who go to the same primary school or play soccer out front, and the area is certainly favored by people with young children, as it is quiet and safe. If there is a typical occupation, it is working as a shop assistant at one of the larger retail centers in the area. Otherwise, there are teachers, school meal attendants, police officers, designers, and researchers, but more commonly we found people engaged in resolutely working-class occupations, such as builders and office staff. Most of those from immigrant families are focused on their children achieving a university education, and mostly they succeed in this. But there are other, more transient immigrants, such as individuals from Eastern Europe looking for summer work. Prices for houses are significantly, though not drastically, lower than average for London.

A few people dissent from the more common nostalgic view of the past and claim that, if anything, the area is friendlier or safer than it used to be. People talk of one or two disruptive families, but largely in the past. The silent community may well represent gradually increasing income levels and associated possessions and a decline in rigid class demarcation. Perhaps the most surprising finding was the parochialism of the few families that have been living here since these streets were first occupied—families for whom it seems as though any journey beyond the local pub still feels like an adventure and who talk about going "to London," meaning to the city center. But apart from a few people who attend the same church, even these do not represent any kind of cohesive community.

People do bemoan the lack of a pub or any other focus of public life. If there is one shift that is seen as particularly negative, it is the rise in the number of properties purchased specifically to be rented out, which are seen as attracting people with even less investment in locality. But in general this is an area where people largely prefer to keep to themselves, where a friendly smile is friendly enough. It is assumed that here, as elsewhere, it doesn't make sense to tempt crime, and that thieving is opportunistic rather than systematic. Elderly people, of whom there are quite a few, seem particularly vulnerable. Yet in practice we were surprised how many people leave their homes empty all day with the windows open. We could certainly confirm the general consensus that this is a "nice enough" area.

Ending this initial chapter with a consideration of the setting also establishes that the study is essentially an ethnography. By the time we have finished describing and analyzing the material from this ethnography, we will have made some radical claims, including the idea that blue jeans represent (as our title suggests) a struggle to become ordinary. But it should be clear from the outset that an ethnography always has to be circumspect about the further process of generalization. We studied blue jeans on three streets. We cannot know how typical those streets are of London; in fact, as we have just seen, there is a whole swath of characteristics quite particular to these streets, as there would be of any three streets in any other part of London. In that sense an ethnography should not be confused with the concept of a sample in the natural sciences. We do not assume the ordinary would play the same role in other parts of the United Kingdom, or in any other country. In fact, the Global Denim Project shows entirely different implications of blue jeans in other parts of the world. None of this, however, diminishes our sense that what we found in those particular three streets has profound significance for understanding foundational concepts within the social sciences. So the generalities found in chapters 7 and 8 are those of social science, not natural science, and they reach toward philosophical issues, not empirical claims as to how the rest of the world relates to blue jeans, which is a matter of comparative anthropology and further studies.

CHAPTER I

Life

If we had simply approached people and asked them to tell us about their jeans, we suspect the response would have been muted. The very clothes-conscious or fashion-aware might have jumped at the chance to engage in detailed discussions of their wardrobes or their opinions on style and fashion. But many others, especially men, might have felt awkward and unnatural, preferring to see clothes as merely something they need to wear but not necessarily make the foreground of conversation. Some older men may hardly ever have been called upon to talk about their clothing, let alone their jeans. In fact, being so focused upon denim in particular comes across as unusual to almost everyone simply because jeans are so ordinary and ubiquitous. Compared to the discussion of more individual or special clothing, jeans just seem rather uninteresting as if it is self-evident and obvious why people should wear them. Our impression was that most participants within the project had barely given their current jeans a second thought after the initial decisions involved in selecting and purchasing them.

Clearly, however, it is a premise of this book that the lack of verbalized discourses around jeans does not mean that they are insignificant. Indeed, both of us were schooled in the writings of Bourdieu (1972), who suggests that such mundane and ubiquitous objects of life (those that have become "second nature") should be regarded as more significant than things whose importance to us we are actively aware of. Given our lack of awareness of these material frames (Goffman 1975), we are less likely to challenge the way in which they structure our lives and expectations. This stance differs considerably from arguments in the social sciences, in part arising from Ricoeur (1987) and more recently expounded by, for example, Lawler (2002), that the narration of a life is part of its examination, and that such narratives are necessarily pivotal to how we make sense of our lives. As Woodward has discussed elsewhere (2010), such expectations fail to acknowledge the extent to which the relationship people have to clothing throughout the life course is largely embodied and material, and subsequently difficult to verbalize. This is especially marked in the case of jeans, our most taken-for-granted garment, whose presence goes without saying.

Consequently, we started out first interviews not with detailed histories of people's jeans but instead we adopted a strategy that concentrated more on a broader, succinct history of the person. Not surprisingly, this is something most people are more than keen to respond to, since in general they rarely encounter anyone with the patience to listen to, let alone continually encourage, these accounts. We did, however, guide such narrations toward the topics we were concerned with: key relationships, the person's broader clothing history, and the place of jeans within these. As a result, it seemed that even those who had started skeptically and claimed they had no time enjoyed the encounter and talked for long periods.

As fieldwork progressed it became increasingly evident that this oscillation between stories of personal lives and the more specific discussion of clothing and jeans seemed to have a kind of natural resonance with informants. Quite aside from our encounter with them, styles of clothing have become increasingly important as ways people mark for themselves certain periods and episodes in their lives. Since the "narrative turn" there has been a move toward the elicitation of life histories, situated within wider social trends (Gullestad 1996; Allan and Jones 2003; Gilleard and Higgs 2005). Clothing is certainly not the only material marker that plays an obvious role here (for autobiography and objects more generally, see Hoskins 1998 and Lofgren 1994), but it is probably the most important. Consider the way we use clothing styles as a rapid means to at least approximately date a family photograph or contextualize a film we are watching. Clothing stands in a special relationship to time, partly because of the strong association with fashion and the temporalities of style, making clothing particularly effective as a temporal marker. As a result, we found that after a while we were able to align our interview technique with this relationship between clothing and the life course in a manner that seemed to work for informants.

In paying attention to such narratives it also becomes clear that this is not simply a very general relationship where clothing becomes a marker of dates or events, standing in for time in general. Furthermore, given the topic, jeans, this was rarely just a story of the degree to which people felt they were in fashion or fashionable. Rather, clothing seems to take on a slightly more abstract or analytical role, in which it stands for a general sense of what people wore during a given period. As we shall see, the key category that marks this relationship between life course and clothing is the concept of generation, particularly for those born in the United Kingdom.

FASHION, PUBLIC NARRATIVES, AND PERSONAL BIOGRAPHY

The potential resonance between a personal life narrative and the history of jeans in particular is exemplified by Eric, now in his seventies, who recalled being given a pair of jeans by an American GI in the mid-1940s. At that time the introduction of jeans into the United Kingdom was closely associated with the presence of American GIs stationed in Britain for the war. It wasn't that he was looking for anything particularly American, but he liked the idea that jeans made him look a bit different. In fact, after a while this seems to have been rather too effective, and he stopped wearing them when he began to feel they marked him out as a bit of an oddball. This is a balance he is still concerned about, in that even today he tries to achieve this sense of being marked out, but not too much, through wearing quirky ties and, curiously, by deliberately not wearing jeans on casual occasions when he knows that other people will be wearing them. So while the initial gift marks a pivotal moment in the original introduction of jeans into the United Kingdom, for him it was simply a means of measuring the extent of his own individuality against that of his contemporaries. Putting this the other way around, we can see that while this is his quite personal and individual trajectory, it was still determined by the public reaction to denim as a historical moment. This is even clearer in the case of a female participant who told us about a relative who in 1958 or 1959 was one of the first women in the area to wear jeans and was promptly beaten up for her effrontery. At such a moment our general statement about the alignment between personal narrative and more-public history seems very apropos.

Rather more common and less dramatic are the ways prevalent styles and fashions become a suitable anchor through which to stabilize auto-biography. Susan was born and brought up locally, working mainly in retail, and now lives with her husband and mother-in-law. She first wore jeans in the mid-1960s, when she was a teenager. She tells us that when she was a child, "my mother never let me wear trousers. I always wore dresses. She desperately wanted a little girl and when she had me she was determined that I wouldn't have trousers." This was in the 1950s, and she therefore became one of those "frilly little girls with bows at their backs." She says that this is what "everyone was wearing—it was no different from anybody else." Her brothers by contrast, wore jeans. She remembers her eldest brother at eleven "desperately wanting jeans. I can remember him having a pair of jeans and he wore it with that snake belt. . . . That was what all the boys wore." This was in the mid-to late 1950s, "around when rock and roll first started." For her, even today wearing jeans still conveys that sense of excitement over a time that, in retrospect, seems like the birth of modern popular culture.

Susan's recollections mainly pertain to her sense of what was in fashion at a given time. When she first wore jeans, "they were the fashion then"; prior to that she wore stretch trousers because "jeans weren't particularly [in fashion], not in the early days. . . . It was at the end of the later sixties when jeans became the fashion for girls." Her first pair of jeans was blue, although "fashion changes so quickly, doesn't it? When I first started wearing them they were blue—but maybe within a year they were colored."

Susan's relationship to jeans occurs within the context of being in tune with fashion. "You know, they were the thing that people were wearing. When you are a teenager you wear whatever everyone else is wearing . . . and so I wore jeans." Fashion dictated not just what you wore but how and when. Jeans were casual wear; "when you went out at the weekend . . . you dressed and you wore dresses. You were a girl and you dressed up." Her sources of fashion knowledge include references to various key films that show 1950s or 1970s style and to Twiggy, an iconic fashion model in the 1960s. It becomes clear that she wanted to "fit in" but also that fashion as a broader concept provided the key explanation and rationalization for what she wore. She exemplifies the classic ambivalences of fashion that Simmel first wrote about in 1904 (Simmel 1957): the tension between standing out and fitting in, between wanting to be noticed yet wanting to wear the same thing as everyone else. She recalls she was a "show-off" when young, and that when she had dressed up in her going-out clothing she wanted people to look at and admire her when she entered a room. Yet this occurs within the context of her sensitivity to keeping within a genre, and fitting in with what others wear. Jeans go even further than other clothing in terms of being different and simultaneously the same, since they start to represent both being in fashion but also the garment that she claims not to care about, precisely because she now sees jeans as a kind of "opting out" from fashion through which she can remain relatively unnoticed. This theme will be developed throughout this book.

Susan's clothing reflects different periods within the life cycle. The unequivocal desire to be in fashion was paramount during her teenage years and her twenties. There was a significant change when Susan got married in 1970 and had a son three years later. Initially she still wore skirts, with jeans mainly as her casual attire, but then she stopped going to discos and instead took to cycling and camping. At this point jeans became her default clothing, what she wore most of the time. By the 1980s she had stopped wearing skirts altogether. She now saw jeans as practical, suitable for her busy life, and the perfect item for when she did not care about her appearance. In the 1990s, however, she stopped wearing denim, and now she wears cotton twill trousers—a transformation she is unable to account for other than on grounds of comfort and habit.

Despite all this, there is no point in her life during which Susan actually regarded jeans as of any special importance or mattering much to her (as was also the case for many other participants). Fashion certainly mattered, as did other activities such as going to discotheques, but jeans come into her narrative precisely as a means of explaining how certain things didn't matter, or mattered less than before. Jeans are used to show how she relinquished her attachment to fashion and relaxed instead into casual clothing. They came into prominence when, with her husband and child, she felt she had other priorities. Yet from the perspective of an analytical engagement with her narrative, one could argue the precise opposite: that jeans were pivotal to her ability to enact these very transformations. They were the means by which she was able to step away from the cycles of fashion, or to be disinterested in clothing while remaining, of course, clothed. So in some ways the less jeans mattered as a genre of fashion, the more they mattered as an instrument of her clothing practice, allowing her to blend in, to be unseen, and not to care about her appearance, or at least to look as if she didn't care.

Again there is an affinity between the place of jeans in our participants' narrative and what we are learning about them. Had we insisted
upon jeans taking center stage in their narrative, it would have seemed
unnatural and uncomfortable. By contrast, accepting jeans as background or context for the discussion of fashion seems to reflect the experience and ultimately the real significance of jeans.

There is often a difference between males and females in the way
clothing and periods of time are aligned. Precisely because Tom does
not have the explicit relationship to fashion declared by Susan, for him
jeans are not merely the "other" to fashion, which means that he has a
more positive and identifiable link to jeans themselves than Susan does.
Tom is from the north of England and has lived in London for fifteen
years. He works as a teacher and lives with his wife and young daughter
and started wearing jeans when he was fourteen. Although his parents
never wore jeans, his mother bought them for him; when he first wore
them he liked them, as they were fashionable. They were different from
school trousers, and it was "what everyone else wore then." He later
clarifies this position by saying that he wasn't "fashionable . . . I
wasn't following trends," yet he also notes that at the time "nobody
wore anything else . . . everyone wore jeans." With Tom, as is typical for
many of our male participants, his ambivalence is slightly different
from that found with Susan. He is less concerned with a relationship to
fashion. Rather, he was a typical male teenager in that his primary concern was simply to fit in. His mother bought Levi's for him, and for a
long time he simply "got into the habit" of wearing them. He wore
flared and then straight-leg jeans in a "very plain" style.

Tom talks about how he loved jeans and how after wearing them for
a while they become more personal: "I felt they were mine." His initial
influences included his peers— "everyone" who was wearing them—as
well as an uncle ten years his senior. Later he developed a sense of himself through a more personal and particular clothing biography. He
shifted from simply fitting in to finding his niche. "I was always behind
the fashions. I had long hair during the punk period. I was grungy during the New Romantic phase. I was always very behind. I didn't worry
about my appearance."

Although Tom claims he doesn't care about his appearance, this is in
respect to what other people wore. By contrast, he showed concern that
his jeans should be aligned with his tastes in music, such as Led Zeppelin, even if they seemed anachronistic. "When I was in the university in
the eighties, to say you were into Pink Floyd was the faux pas. Everyone

else was into New Romantics. Pink Floyd were definitely out." Similarly, the flared jeans he wore, which seemed appropriate when listening to such music, were clearly out of fashion: "I wore flares until I was laughed at on the streets. . . . I can remember being in the university in flares and some local kids laughing as I went past."

This experience seems to have become, in his memory, the turning point. He bought a pair of straight-leg jeans and stopped wearing flares. Still, clearly the issue of jeans was secondary to his deep relationship with music. He tells how he wished he had been born fifteen years earlier: "It wasn't deliberately trying to stand out. It was just knowing the sort of music I liked."

It would seem misleading to consider Tom in relation to any general sense of fashion. What remains consistent is his concern with fitting in. At first the contradiction was expressed by wanting to look right for the small subgroup that shared his musical tastes, but then gradually he was confronted with the discrepancy between this group and everyone else, culminating in his being laughed at in the street, at which point he shifted back to conformity with a larger public. Similarly, when he subsequently obtained a job as a teacher he started wearing cords rather than jeans, which are not allowed at work. But he also welcomed these cords, which gave him a sense of himself as more "grown-up." Once he stopped wearing jeans, denim as a material started to seem too harsh and the cut of jeans too restrictive to his body. He now only wears chinos.

If in the case of Tom it is music that mediates between jeans and the period he is living through, for most participants this mediation comes through a generally very broad sense of fashion. In short, they don't see themselves in terms of specific linkages to jeans. More often they recall the past in terms of a general age bracket associated with a particular decade. Tom talks about the way he, like others, took to wearing flared jeans in the 1970s or combats—loose cotton military-style trousers with large pockets that were popular in the UK in the 1990s. For him this goes with the way he converses about the music of bands from the seventies or eighties; others see it as natural to frame their sartorial biographies in terms of clothes from the 1960s or the 1990s.

To generalize from Tom and many other participants, jeans are subsumed within narrations based on a general correspondence (or sometimes a failure of correspondence) to a broad-brush sense of changes in style over time. The key term here is *generation*. There is an extensive academic debate over this term: Allan and Jones (2003), for example, prefer to use *cohort,* as *generation* is linked to kinship. But *cohort* has its own problems and is, moreover, less colloquial. Taking our cue from the ethnography, we see a generation not just in terms of people born around the same time but also as an affinity and memory with respect to music and clothing in particular (see also Corsten 1999). These are not just issues of style; they are defined by the way people behaved at that time, as well as by wider social changes and aspirations. It is this that allows Tom to think of himself as belonging more naturally to a generation different from the one he is actually living in. The point is not at all that the people we interviewed were necessarily wearing the same kinds of clothing at the same time, but rather that they showed a common reference point through their sense of what was normative with respect to that period.

CRISIS AND CONSERVATISM

It also follows that even though people may care very little about clothing or their relationship to clothing, they can still generally narrate both a personal clothing life history and a general clothing life history that in turn speaks to wider social changes and to shifts in their own life. In some cases, especially for women, this may be grounded in their concept of fashion; in other cases, as with Tom, it is based more on a sense of fitting in. Another dimension to these narratives is shifts between periods of conservatism or consolidation and those characterized by rupture and change. This is where more particular and personal circumstances intrude, such as changes in body shape or key relationships. The evidence largely conforms to the conclusions of Woodward's previous ethnography of women's wardrobes (2007) and the way individuals come to a sense of who they are and "what is me" through the externalization of the self as an aesthetic form. For some this continues to shift throughout their life, while for others there emerges a much clearer sense of stability; their clothing style plateaus once they reach adulthood and what they regard as a mature sense of who they have now become.

This process can be expressed as a kind of entrenched or inbuilt conservatism in taste, as exemplified in two further cases. Farid, in his thirties and of mixed Indian and Iranian parentage, says, "I've always been stuck in the sixties." He grew up watching Michael Cain, Steve McQueen, and Sean Connery films, and as a result he has become very attached to a 1960s "Mod" style of dressing. He wears jeans around half of the time, yet almost always black jeans (which are not particularly common, at least as compared to blue). He prefers the slim-leg cut that corresponds to this Mod style. There are evident similarities to Tom, who also chose a clothing style associated with people of a generation different from his own. However, unlike Tom's, Farid's style is not considered unfashionable, and is relatively unmarked and unnoticed. Mod style can work as a kind of classic mode and is an acceptable point of recurrent reference, even if in practice, as with most "classic" styles, it changes each time it is resurrected.

A more marked conservatism is evident in the case of Dilip, now in his seventies, who only briefly wore jeans when he was much younger. But by the time they were fashionable he had a wife, children, and a "bit of a paunch." Despite the fact that he has lived in the United Kingdom since 1952, the style of brown trousers and white shirt that he wears day in and day out would be instantly recognizable to anyone who has spent any time in India. Both Dilip and Farid adopted a clothing style when quite young that they have retained thereafter. This idea that one reaches a plateau that becomes the sartorial foundation for who a person subsequently remains is more often true of those over forty, but it is also found with younger participants. A variant is found in Tom's series of transitions from flared jeans to straight-leg ones, cords, and then chinos; it results from his sense of certain styles being "age-appropriate." The norm or at least the expectation is that people will experiment with clothing styles when young, making all their fashion faux pas at that time. What is less clear is the subsequent norm, which may include further but more muted experimentation, just keeping up with wider trends, or entirely opting out of any resonance with the changing world of contemporary fashion.

Jeans can become the epitome of this conservatism and stability in style, allowing someone to remain relatively unnoticed. Jeans may also act as a break from style. The theorization of clothing that we both subscribe to (Miller 2010, 12–41; Woodward 2007) is not one in which clothes are thought of as primarily semiotic—that is, a reflection of something about the person or an act of representation. Rather, in material culture studies clothing is seen more as an active agent or instrument, as it is a means by which people accomplish various tasks, including that of dealing with a difficult situation; in some cases as a catalyst that provokes further change. This is perhaps clearest in instances in these life narratives when people have used jeans as a kind of resource for helping them in responding to a crisis or major change in their lives. An example would be Tom's wife, Pauline, talking about her parents' divorce.

When she was growing up, neither of her parents wore jeans, even though their friends did. But "later in life my father did hit the point—he went through a phase of wearing jeans. He's come out at the other end now—he's back to what he used to wear now. He did go through a phase, after my mother left, so it was very upsetting." That was when he was in his forties. "It was a very unsettled period in his life." She thinks maybe the "new woman" bought them for him. She also notes that he started doing other new things, such as going on holidays, "which he never did with my mother." Now he has stopped wearing jeans. Pauline talks about her father going through a "phase," rather in the manner of a naughty teenager, where jeans are viewed as an act of rebellion, or at least something one might turn to at a moment of change and crisis. Similarly, her mother wore jeans for the first time after the split; Pauline went with her to buy some in Debenhams, as her mother had been ill and lost weight. She also tried on a range of new clothes and other styles. She was, in Pauline's words, "reliving her youth." For Pauline's parents, jeans are linked not to stability but to turning points in their lives. Far from being unmarked and helping people remain unnoticed, jeans are viewed as a means to help people become visible again. More particularly, these two individuals, who never wore jeans when they were younger, now see jeans as being linked to youth, which in turn has associations with being fickle and changing clothing styles.

An additional contrast between Pauline's parents and the other examples was that the rupture with previous clothing styles came through a major shift in personal relationships rather than through some more generic link to style, period, or music. This is often the case, but not necessarily. People can also talk in terms of rupture and radical change even when this remains within the idiom of personal development related to general shifts in one's circumstance or the background sartorial culture. David lived in Brixton until he was sixteen before moving to this street, where he has lived ever since. His parents are Hong Kong Chinese. As a youth he wore baggy, hip-hop-style jeans, and hung out on the street with his friends, who were mainly black. Riding his BMX, he cultivated a "bad-boy look." But following the move to North London and to a different school with a larger British Chinese population, combined with a visit to Hong Kong and finding himself quite taken with the place, he started to feel more Chinese and proud of his heritage. He began to wear fitted "plain" jeans. He was looking not for a Chinese form of dress, as he still defined himself as British, but for something that fit his sense of this British Chinese milieu. He has stuck with jeans ever since, and they have become the mainstay of his casual clothing (though he has gone through subtle shifts in the precise style of jeans). For David, jeans became a medium through which he could negotiate changes in how he saw himself relative to others, and as a means to articulate his feelings of belonging and a deeper sense of himself.

BODY AND BIOGRAPHY

For David, the changes were in his social environment. By contrast, for many women the changes they are negotiating are much more related to their bodies—the "problems" they see themselves as confronting or coming to terms with. Pauline provides good evidence of this. She describes herself as wearing jeans until she put on weight, at which point she felt they weren't as comfortable. "I always wore them as a child" and then through university. "I guess the key change came with getting a job, really. At the same time as getting the job I also did put weight on then." She says now she looks at the size 10s and 12s "and I think they look gorgeous, and then you look at the size 18s and you think . . . no." Many other women we spoke to, and also some men, had similar stories about how once they became a certain weight they no longer wore jeans. For others, losing weight allows them to wear jeans. Mickala, a slim woman in her late twenties, is married and has a small child. She was born in London to a Filipina mother and white English father; she didn't wear jeans as a child. "I was quite a fat kid. . . . I only started wearing jeans when the low-cuts came out . . . and when I lost weight."

In primary school she wore dresses, which her mother gave her (her mother wears lots of "awful flowery dresses"), and she went through a phase of wearing leggings. She started wearing jeans after leaving secondary school and going into college. She remembers Mariah Carey in her "Heartbreaker" video wearing them; they were low-cut, "and I thought, 'Oh God, if they look like that . . . !' " She started buying her own clothes in this period, ones completely different from those her mother would wear or buy for her. As is common for teenagers, she used the money from her first part-time jobs to assert her independence through a repudiation of her mother's taste. She says that at first she "lost weight, but I was still a bit chubby, so I didn't wear them sexy, I just wore them with T-shirts." Initially she preferred black jeans, but gradually she lost more weight, and now she wears blue jeans. She too claims blue jeans make her more visible. She "lived in Jane Norman . . . I liked the way their jeans and stuff fit. I found when I went to New Look that their sizing was really funny. I didn't like their cut. That and River Island. I stuck to them."

Now that Mickala has a baby she no longer goes clubbing, so she wears jeans all the time. She has gone down to a size 6, as she is always running around after her baby. Many of her jeans don't fit her now. "I don't have a butt, so I need stuff to hold me," she says; otherwise, she feels, she looks terrible. Concerned about being too skinny, she says, "I like fitted jeans because I look skinny and weird with big baggy jeans. I always go for quite fitted jeans."

> I can wear a skirt and I look buttless. I wear jeans from the right shop like Jane Norman and they're low cut and . . . they create this body shape that you don't have. . . . For me the bum's more important that anything else. I won't buy jeans it if gives me a flat bum. So many of them just squash it right in, and I hate that look. . . . I always check if my bum looks good in the jeans . . . they always go really bad around the bum. They really sag on me.

As Mickala tells these stories, it is clear how at each stage in her life she sees a close relationship between her jeans and changes in her body; those changes come to entirely dominate her jeans wearing. As is evident from these selections of narrative, it isn't always a case of finding jeans to fit her body; more often she has a sense that her body needs to change shape in order to go with jeans. Jeans are both the measure of her body and sometimes even the reward for getting her body shape right. She is not necessarily typical, but she is certainly not unique, either. Many of our informants feel that they need a slim enough body to fit the look of jeans; yet once they have this type of body, there is a sense that jeans are supposed to "do" something for the wearers, whether give them a bottom or hide a stomach. A sort of magical agency is attributed to jeans. While this is less evident in London, Sassatelli (2011) in her work in Milan found a close correspondence between this concept of fit (that is, getting the physical relationship between jeans and the body right in terms of tightness or baginess) and how the clothed body in this process becomes sexualized.

CONCLUSION

In our initial encounters with participants, we asked them to talk about their lives in a concise biography and this chapter has explored the ways in which jeans work within this life history. One of the key issues to emerge was that of "generation" in terms of what people wore in certain periods of their life and also what was more broadly fashionable at any one period. This sense of change within people's lives and as they located themselves in wider social histories was for many mediated through music and clothing. Jeans can here be understood as linking the individual to wider social groups and time periods and also broader sartorial change. Within these life histories jeans also work in terms of people's sense of themselves, both in relationship to periods of time and a consequent sense of stability, change, or rupture, and also in their wider relationships—to style in general, to other people, and finally to themselves in terms of their own bodies.

For some people, wearing jeans is a constant in their lives; whilst others have had periods of not wearing them at all. Jeans occupy a seemingly contradictory relationship to change and continuity, as they may allow for a consistent identity or for others the wearing or rejection of them allows a change in status or self-conception. For some, jeans are a means of managing changes, in the extreme something they turn to at moments of crisis. Overall we confront at this stage in our discussion a quite bewildering pattern of what jeans could mean in relationship to people's life history. It is already evident that there are going to be few easy or consistent answers to the question of what jeans mean and what they do for people. We have seen many examples of ambivalence and contradiction with respect to jeans wearing.

All of these elements will be developed further during the course of this volume. The theme that remains closest to the specific issues of jeans in the life course is this concept of generation, and the way it assists people in reflecting back on the clothing they wore in particular periods of their life. It was evident jeans form part of a much wider context, including music and clothing more generally but also other markers such as popular TV series that were shown during those years. Yet we might have expected this to be connected to jeans more in terms of fashion. Certainly informants could relate specific styles of jeans they were associated with at such times, such as bell-bottoms or drainpipes. But while these may be related to prevalent styles of clothing, the term *fashion* or the idea of fashion was not the key link between jeans and period. Fashion seems to play other roles, and in chapter 3 we will look more closely at this relationship between fashion, style, and jeans.

Another tentative area that we will explore more deeply as we proceed involves the various forms of ambivalence that have emerged around jeans wearing. A key example is just how much their jeans mattered to our participants. Many people talk about having worn jeans most at the point in their life when they didn't care about clothing. When they were too busy with other concerns to think about what to wear, jeans were perfect to just "get on with things." For others (albeit far fewer), the interview was a catalyst for their appreciation of jeans as having been very important at particular stages of their life. The fact that this acknowledgment seems to have emerged largely through the process of being interviewed confirms a more general impression of jeans as something best considered as background rather than foreground. In a manner that echoes our earlier discussion of Bourdieu, people come to appreciate that something played a significant role in their lives precisely because this occurred through a shift in practice rather than a more self-conscious or explicit strategy on their part. When we consider jeans as a backdrop, the seeming paradox that most people wear jeans and have done so throughout their lives yet appear not to care or have thought about them a great deal starts to become explicable.

Similarly, jeans are already emerging as something that can be understood as quite impersonal and generic, a garment that allows a person to escape notice or blend in. Yet we are also seeing the first evidence that they can simultaneously be deeply personal and intimate. Overall, it is not surprising that asking people to talk about their life course tends to elicit aspects of their relationship to jeans that have a great deal to do with their personal development. Yet it is already clear that much of this personal development is embedded in relationships to others, both particular others and more general social movements and trends. The book will follow this movement from the individual to such wider relationships: in the next chapter by considering personal relationships and the household, and in later chapters fashion and broader movements of people, such as the experiences of immigrants.

CHAPTER 2

Relationships

It is apparent from the last chapter that a clothing biography is never entirely personal. Life histories through clothing always draw in relationships to others, such as parents, siblings, and peer groups. These are present both as more generalized influences upon an individual's life and through specific stories, interactions, and memories. Two points of intersection are particularly prominent: stories of how clothing is gifted, borrowed, or passed on by others (Clarke 2000; Corrigan 1995; Woodward 2007) and constant reference to the opinions of others as to how a person looks in his or her clothes. The case study of David, in the last chapter, took note of this shifting influence of his various groups of friends upon his sense of himself and his jeans.

Although we initiated many of our interviews with a request for personal narratives, we also always intended to try to find ways through which a study of three streets in London, where most people have no idea who their neighbors are, could also be given a more ethnographic complexion. For this reason, during the course of the research we interviewed nine sets of people who lived in the same household and/or were connected to each other. Of these, three were heterosexual married couples, three were mothers and daughters, one was a father and his two sons, one was a mother and her son, and one was a couple of friends who lived together (we also interviewed their landlord, who owned a few houses on the street). One of the mother-daughter groups also included a sister-in-law, and another included a cousin who lived in another house on the street. We thereby managed to locate a range of different types of relationship and associations, which allowed the same individual to come up in different people's narratives (one of the defining features of traditional ethnography). These relationships and choices of informant arose quite naturally through someone volunteering a friend or relative as we came to know them a little better.

In this chapter we start by looking at the key initial influences within the household, which is often that of parents over children. We then look to other relationships, both those of couples and those of friendships.* These continue and build upon the idea of jeans in relation to the life course but also introduce new and different dimensions to people's relationship with jeans. Part of our particular version of material culture studies is that when undertaking such research we try to avoid any presumptions about the significance or salience of social parameters such as class, ethnicity, or gender. We feel there is a danger that if one seeks out such categories, then little is gained by the claim to have found them to be significant. We would rather be open to the possible finding that such dimensions of difference are unimportant for our particular topic of inquiry. But we certainly intend to acknowledge their salience where our evidence supports this. With respect to the topic of this chapter, issues of gender emerged as of particular importance in the context of relationships. We found that the relationships that are constructed and maintained through clothing are also crucially constructed through gender: either through gender differentiation or complementarity or through gradations of, for example, masculinity being defined through friendship groups.

PARENTS AND CHILDREN

One of the advantages of material culture research is that relationships often emerge through observations of people and their clothes while the people remain silent, either because they are not conscious of the influence of those relationships or because they prefer not to acknowledge that influence. This is especially likely in the subtle, often fraught relationships between parents and children. For example, a father lives with his new partner and one of his two sons; the other, Darren, we interviewed

---

* In this particular street study, no one presented themselves as other than heterosexual, which was a clear contrast with Miller (2008) where homosexual couples were a common feature.

when he was visiting. Darren has a striking physical resemblance to the father, not just in looks but also in manner and demeanor. When we met him he was wearing a pair of faded black jeans and a red T-shirt that he borrowed from his father. He is now eighteen and wears jeans as casual attire. He told us a story about the first pair of jeans he bought when he was younger: a pair of Levi's, which cost £89 at a time when he was only earning £50 a week from a part-time job. He progressed through a range of styles, as is typical of teenagers experimenting with clothes, trying on skinny, tighter jeans; now he wears just "regular" jeans. There has been a more general shift in his clothes in the last couple of years, as he now often wears a suit to go out in, which he relates to his love of 1950s swing music (such as by Frank Sinatra and Bobby Darin).

Darren recognizes that wearing this kind of suit makes him stand out; as he puts it, "I know it's not that normal." Having this relatively nonconformist side to his sartorial life may well account for his current predilection for regular jeans, making a kind of overall balance. His jeans must therefore be considered in relationship to the rest of his wardrobe, as different categories and types of clothing serve different functions within his life. The concept of wardrobe will be important throughout this chapter, as the reasons people have for wearing jeans will always in some sense be relative to the other clothing choices available to them. Darren is typical of many informants in that the meaning jeans have for him comes from the contrast with the clothing he wears at other times, differences that help him compartmentalize his life into appropriate domains. The first time he met his current girlfriend, for example, he was wearing sports gear, since he had just come from playing soccer; the second time they went out, he wore jeans, and the third time he wore a suit, which she told him she much prefers. Her approval served to cement his attachment to wearing suits whenever he goes out (though he will also now go to a party wearing the jacket from his suits combined with jeans, having previously checked out this combination with his girlfriend). His father talks about this change in his son's clothing as deriving from the father's own taste in music and specifically from about three years ago when they went on vacation together to Fuerteventura, in the Canary Islands. He has a friend who sings swing jazz, and his son really took to the associated style, consisting of "black trousers, black shoes, black shirt with a white tie, white braces."

The father has a clear influence on Darren that extends beyond music and clothes. His son also briefly had a go at motorcycling, his father's enduring passion. Darren's father was bought up in Watford, and when he was younger everyone wore jeans. He wore them to ride his motorcycle, as he couldn't afford proper leathers at the time. He also used to wear jeans and a leather jacket with a white T-shirt as regular attire. He talks about the influence of music (bands such as Led Zeppelin and Whitesnake) and the "rocker look." He didn't really care about the jeans as long as they weren't new-looking and were a bit battered. He turned his passion for bikes into his job for a while, as he worked for the Royal Automobile Club motorcycle display team fixing bikes. Once he was working he could afford proper motorcycle leathers.

So although there are clear points of difference between Darren and his father in that Darren never went as far as wearing leathers for motorcycle riding (never being that serious about it), there are also continuities. Darren's father says of his son that when he goes out he looks very different from his crowd of friends. He "can be a bit strange, but then he's an exact copy of me . . . though I won't go that far, I'll sort of go out a bit different." So Darren's father, too, had in his own time been prepared to look different to a certain degree. An example he recalls is when he used to go out wearing blue jeans and a blue denim waistcoat over the top of the black leather jacket. For Darren's father, contrasting denim with his other clothing was the basis for giving himself alternative looks. He therefore has a different relationship to jeans than his son does: rather than denim being a medium of blending in or of not caring, for Darren's father it is worn as a statement: "It's a heavy sort of 'I'm going to a rock concert, I'm riding my motorcycle with a group of motorcyclists.'" He sees Darren as continuing this trait of looking different but recognizes that his son has in effect taken this a good deal further simply because certain styles look far more conspicuous when worn by someone of Darren's generation than by someone of his father's. By contrast, when Darren's father wore denim it was to engineer a more idiosyncratic look, while for his son it is a sign of conformity. For Darren's father, even if denim allows him to blend in, combining it with other items in his wardrobe in certain ways allows him to differentiate himself. (This is an issue that will be developed later in the book.) All of this emerges from conversations with Darren's father; it is not an influence that Darren himself refers to at all. But it is clearly confirmed by our observations of Darren's clothing.

A still more striking affinity between parent and child was evident in the case of Hema and her mother. The latter, now forty-eight years old, was born in Sri Lanka but moved to the United Kingdom to marry. She has lived on the street for twenty-one years, currently with her two children, husband, and mother-in-law. In addition, there are several other family members living on the street or in the nearby area. We interviewed the mother and daughter together, as this was their preference and as Hema was only sixteen. The close relationship between them was obvious, as they held hands at times or had their arms casually draped around each other. Hema is quite shy and on occasion says just one word as a trigger; her mother then completes the sentence, and Hema nods her agreement. They also look very alike, being exceptionally petite.

Both of them constantly wear jeans; Hema's mother prefers jeans to almost anything else. It's not a case of just wearing jeans by default, as is the case with so many others; she is actually quite passionate about them. Growing up in Sri Lanka with six brothers, she usually had to wear dresses, but she talks about longing to wear trousers. She only really started wearing jeans about twenty years ago, but in the last ten years she has "lived" in them, and only on very formal occasions does she wear a sari. In common with Darren, for Hema's mother jeans form a contrast to other clothing in her wardrobe. As Woodward outlined in her in-depth study of women's wardrobes (2007), categories of clothing acquire their meaning through their relationship to the other items in the wardrobe. This may be through contrast, as when jeans come to feel more relaxed or casual in contrast to more dressy going-out clothing. But many people have several pairs of jeans in their wardrobe, which broadens the potential combinations and contrasts. Woodward argued that jeans mediate the categories of "habitual" and "nonhabitual" clothing, as women both know how to wear them and feel comfortable in them, yet also use this foundation to allow themselves to stand out and experiment with their look. What is apparent from this wider ethnography of people's relationship to their jeans is that this is a spectrum. Some people value jeans exclusively for the unselfconscious relationship they have to wearing them.

Returning to Hema's mother, she always "wears the fashions." She hates straight-leg jeans as being "out of fashion," and she wears skinny jeans even though by her own admission they leave her with "chicken legs." She says her brothers and family often utter a bemused sigh to indicate that she really doesn't dress her age. In fact, at most parties she readily wears jeans with, for example, a halter-neck top, the very same kind of top that her teenage niece has been wearing to the same occasions. Hema notes what her mother is wearing or what is in her wardrobe. She takes stock of which ones she likes, and on occasion her mother will then buy these for her daughter in a smaller size. This is not entirely straightforward, as Hema is a size 4 or 6. They have the same camisole tops, one in black and the other in white; neither minds if they wear them at the same time. Hema's mother notes that other people may comment about this: "They say, 'You've got to grow up, you can't wear your daughter's.' . . . Why not?" She claims that even Hema has said, "Mum, you have to look like a mum,'" but then Hema interjects, "One time she dressed like her age and she had a bun and she looked disgusting." In fact, Hema says she prefers her mother looking a bit younger, and she says that for the next two years her mother can dress in young stuff like her, but "after I turn eighteen she has to stop." The mother swiftly retorts, "That is what she thinks!" Clearly this forms part of the everyday banter between a mother and daughter who feel particularly close. But there is still that ambivalence, at least for Hema, who on one hand seems to like the way her mother can look young and who doesn't particularly want to have to get used to an "old" mother or even an "age-appropriate" mother, but who on the other hand shows a growing awareness of the normative expectations of what a mother "should" look like and how she should behave. But she worries about the way this would redefine their relationship and possibly disrupt it.

Generally Hema and her mother celebrate the way their clothing tastes reflect the overall closeness of their relationship: they shop together and spend their leisure time together. Although Hema also has jeans sent to her by family in Canada, she refuses to wear any of these and says that she doesn't like the styles: "I have to be there to choose my own jeans." Unlike her mother, she does not dress in whatever the current fashion is, and she won't wear skinny jeans or anything too flashy. Contrary to the more common pattern, in which it is the young person who is concerned about following fashion, it is Hema's mother who expresses such concerns. By contrast, it is Hema who emphasizes the more practical aspects of jeans and her desire to keep her treasured pairs of jeans as long as possible. Hema talks with some sadness of one pair that she used to "live" in, but they ripped at the fly. Hema wanted her mother to fix them for her, but her mother said she couldn't do it: "You need the right needle . . . and you can't just sew it by hand, you need to run it through the machine . . . and you need the right thread."

These two stories are typical of parent-child relationships in that they reflect, in different ways, an ambivalence between continuity and separation, acknowledgment and repudiation (for an expansion of this point, see Miller 1997). This is one of the reasons our evidence needs to come as much from careful observation of the clothes as from anything that anyone says. In the case of Hema, the emphasis is on friendly banter and mutual regard, but elsewhere we could observe tension and even coercion that reflected the common issues of the teenage years with their struggles for autonomy. Indeed, there was a time historically when jeans were the quintessential signifiers of just this tension, as portrayed in the now iconic wearing of jeans by film stars such as James Dean and Marlon Brandon.

The more coercive version of this relationship was illustrated by Fatima, who was born in Pakistan, the youngest of three sisters and five brothers, and grew up, in her own words, as a "tomboy." Her mother started telling her at eighteen that she worried about her wearing jeans, as they were too tight. "She didn't want me to wear very revealing ones. Because I did start getting a bit bulky from the hips." The mother started by persuading Fatima to cover up a bit more. In the end, though, it was one of her brothers who said to her, "You're getting too big. You shouldn't be wearing really tight jeans." In fact, she didn't stop wearing them until she was married at twenty-four and her husband told her, "You look really bad in them." His influence was enough to finally stop her from wearing them.

We are social scientists rather than psychologists, but there may well be a relationship between these sources of external discipline and the subsequent, often almost obsessive concerns many women in particular seem to develop about their body. Fatima talks freely about her body size and how this affects what she can wear. It is a constant source of concern and discussion between her and her two sisters, who both live nearby. She says she never really "needed friends," as she always had her sisters, and they remain very close. They talk about their respective concerns with their bodies "all of the time"—how they are unable to wear the clothes they used to. All three struggle with their weight, and none of them feels able to wear jeans. One still keeps a size 8 pair in her wardrobe (she is a size 14 now) and says that "jeans are the reward" for losing weight. What this example demonstrates is the difficulty of expecting any clear point of demarcation between individual preference, as discussed in the last chapter, and the influence of others, as highlighted in this chapter. This reinforces a theme common to both psychology and anthropology: individual preference is often the internalized authority of others or of social norms more generally.

In these previous cases the issue has been either parental control or parental influence, with a subsidiary impact from siblings. But there is another dimension to these intrahousehold relationships that emanates from the direct giving or sharing of clothes between household members. Janice is originally from Wales, one of eleven children. Her life was essentially rural before she moved to London as a teenager. Janice had six older siblings and lived in a family where clothes were constantly being passed down to younger siblings. Although her jeans only ever came from her sisters, she used her association with an outdoor life, in which she climbed trees and rode scooters, to frame herself as a tomboy. She would change into jeans after school, and bought her first pair when she was sixteen and had started working. Even now that she has two grown daughters, she still has jeans "handed up" to her by one daughter who is twenty-two but is almost the same size. Her daughter buys "expensive" jeans for about £60, and when they are passed up to Janice, she says she does not discriminate between these and her own cheaper jeans. "Jeans are just jeans," she says; she cannot tell the difference between pairs of different prices and quality.

One male informant told us that after having bought several new pairs of jeans, he subsequently put on so much weight that he was forced to pass them down to his son; much to the boy's delight, they happened to fit perfectly. Commonly this is something that people recall from when they were younger. For example, Peggy, who is now sixty, remembers how she and her friends used to wear their male friends' jeans. This was not a particular fashion of the time, as far as she was aware, but just something they did in order to look "different." Jeans were only casual wear; when they went out, they dressed up in skirts. So they did not see this as an explicit challenge to gender or femininity. It was more likely that, as in some of the cases described in the previous chapter, they expressed a desire to refute choices imposed on them by their parents. This most often emerges as a refusal to wear "girly" or feminine clothes that represented their mothers' projections onto them. An example was Radka, a young Czech women who lived on the street for the summer in a house share so that she could save some money for her studies. She was brought up by her grandmother, as her parents had divorced, and was made to wear very girly clothing. She now always wears jeans that are either baggy or loose-fitting, and she professes to have an aversion to the color pink. Often these struggles remain as a legacy after individuals have left home. Woodward (2011) has elsewhere analyzed the contemporary phenomenon of women wearing their boyfriend's jeans as a way of dressing in relationship to others, and sometimes as a means by which women can negotiate the fragility of those relationships. As it happens, we did not encounter this phenomenon in our work for this ethnography. But there is evident continuity between that and these various instances of hand-me-downs and the sharing of jeans.

ESTABLISHING HOUSEHOLDS

This progression from parental control to wider public conformity is expressed not just in self-discipline but also in the increasingly important relationship to peers. In clothing as elsewhere, the supposed experimentations of the teenage years are also characterized by a strong level of conformity. When Janine goes out she tends to always go first to a friend's house to get ready, as she and her friends share opinions on each other's outfits—skirts and dresses to go out in. Her mother still gives her opinion, but increasingly Janine turns to friends. "They are the ones. . . . It is the fact that people will judge you . . . the ones you are going to be associating with." These friends happen to work in the beauty industry, and that gives her confidence in their views. She has one friend with whom she shares similar tastes, and she talks of others who are "really cool": one who is understated, another who is "wacky," another who is a "throwback from the eighties," another who is "punky." She paints a picture of a wide range of styles but says, "I don't put myself into a certain group. . . . I'm a bit mixed. That's why I might wear jeans with trainers and then another day skinny jeans with rock-type trainers . . . but jeans are always there no matter how I dress." We can start to see here a pattern whereby jeans seem to assist in this oscillation between style and conformity, experimentation and safety. This continues even when her peer group expands to include people as diverse as chavs and Goths, since they still all wear jeans, which become the common ground from which one can start to explore other, less familiar aspects of these groups.* Such concern over friends and peers is, unsurprisingly, particularly pertinent for teenagers. For instance, Ches, a sixteen-year-old girl, lives with her mother, as her parents have split up. The impact of her peers is evident not just from what she says but also from the outfit she wears to her first interview: skinny jeans and Ugg boots, entirely in fashion with her peers at the time.

As teenagers grow older, the peer group may become more diverse, and there may be still more emphasis upon creating an individual style

---

* The term *chavs* refers to a low-income, low-education British subculture, the members of which may aggressively sport styles that are regarded as vulgar by more privileged classes.

that nevertheless retains its adherence to a larger sense of commonality. This is evident in the relationship between Joe and George, two nineteen-year-olds, both originally from Australia, who share a rented house. They regret the fact that this district is so removed from the kind of party world they want to spend their time in, but they still manage to replicate a kind of post-student laid-back house interior strewn with random possessions. They were at primary school together and came over to England together. In Australia they mainly wore shorts. Joe first wore jeans at about twelve, in a "rock star" look, with big baggy jeans, as his parents instilled a love of rock and roll in him. His parents wore classic straight-leg jeans. Whenever we talk to Joe, he can't keep still and is leaping around or playing distractedly with something in his hand. He has disheveled curly hair that falls over his shoulders; he currently works in construction and is wearing a pair of faded, dirty blue jeans that are slightly ripped. He owns four pairs of jeans—black, two grays, and the blue ones—and tends to wear tighter, stretchier jeans to go out in. He describes his going-out ensemble as consisting of black Converses, tight jeans, and shirts that are loose-fitting (but not too loose). He has cultivated this style over the last four or five years. He goes into central London "If there's a band on or a gig." He dresses both to attract women and to "feel good."

By contrast, George is conspicuously tall (six feet six inches), a fact of which he is very self-conscious. He wears straight-leg jeans. "I don't like tight ones. But not too baggy." He started buying his own jeans at about fourteen. He wasn't after any special look. He "didn't really have a clique. I didn't like them tight like Joe does. And not baggy. Just straight-leg . . . When I was younger I think baggy ones were quite popular. Like a size too big. But I didn't like it. But I didn't want them tighter . . . I just don't like the look. It probably wouldn't suit me as well. But I also don't like it." He is very keen to not dress in any extremes, as if to compensate for his height. On drainpipe jeans, he says, "I reckon it looks fine on Joe, in all honesty. It's just not something I'd fancy wearing." Although he refers to the look as "metrosexual," he later changes his mind. He certainly doesn't see himself as metrosexual, he would never wear pink, and doesn't want to be seen as someone particularly devoted to clothes: "I do care about how I look but not heaps." It's important that he doesn't actually look as though he has made much of an effort "because I don't. I don't spend ages. I don't contemplate it. I just open my cupboard, grab whatever, if it's clean . . . and just go." In many ways he is trying to work out what a "typical" guy is and attempting to enact this normative position. He is reluctant and even a bit embarrassed to be talking about clothes, as if he feels he would rather exemplify the "unseen" that seems to fit in with the normative idea of taken-for-granted masculinity. He clearly contrasts his own style to that of Joe, who "wears a lot of headbands and he has curly hair and it attracts a lot of attention. And his personality attracts a lot of attention. He's come close to getting his head knocked off. We're always like, 'Joe, calm down.' He never recalls any of it. He's one of those people you always have to keep an eye on. But don't tell him that."

What this example highlights, as did many others, is how gender is defined through, and in part constructs, these relationships. Gender itself was not an explicit focus of inquiry, but it became increasingly significant as the research progressed, especially as an aspect of relationships. This was very evident in the previous discussion of parent-child relationships, in which children may be socialized into highly gendered norms (Holland and Adkins 1996; Mann 1996) against which they often rebel, rejecting, for example, "girly" clothes.

Gender is an evident feature in relationships between heterosexual couples. But even with Joe and George we can see how they are developing different but complementary images of masculinity, which they measure through their friendship. There is a wider literature recognizing the gendering of consumption and in particular fashion, mainly in terms of the way these have been historically feminized, and the contemporary legacy (Bell and Hollows 2005; De Grazia and Furlough 1996; Hollows 2000; Lury 1996). But more recently there have been arguments that in the last two decades of the twentieth century there has been an increased shift toward linking of forms of masculinity with consumption and pleasure (Edwards 2005; Mort 1996).

Joe and George are helpful in showing that this does not require us to assume that men are explicitly identifying themselves with fashion or becoming overtly or overly concerned with their appearance. It can still be the case that clothing emerges as important in terms of how they enact and practice their sense of masculinity. Many authors have pointed toward such variant and multiple "masculinities" (Connell 2005; Haywood and Mac an Ghaill 2003; Whitehead and Barrett 2001). Joe's look can develop individually even to the point of eccentricity yet still remain within the parameters that jeans construct, which ensure that he is still seen as "straight" and as a "regular guy." The contrast was also clear when we came to work with their landlord, who does not live on the street but agreed to be interviewed. He was much more explicit about trying to be "laddish," flirting with both Sophie and Sabrina, making jokes about smoking a spliff, and asking them to confirm how "fit" his wife is. Joe and George were clearly embarrassed by the crudeness of all this. They see their sartorial stances as more subtle and effective ways of creating a space for individualism and difference within a more relaxed and therefore effective mode of gendered style.

Taking our work as a whole, we can see the movement from parental and intrahousehold influences upon children to the rise of teenagers with their peers and the cultivation of gendered stereotypes. The next stage is when individuals become increasingly oriented to attracting a partner, leading to the formation of couples and the setting up of new households. What emerges in these latter stages is a pattern in which the complementarity within the couple itself becomes central to the way people either conform to a wider homogeneity of style or accede to the pressure to develop a more individual or idiosyncratic style. Feminist positions that see gender as relational (arising out of specific contexts, including both people and relationships) and in particular as an expression of difference have been critiqued by Butler, who argues that this assumes "oppositional heterosexuality" (1999, 31). In this book we are attempting not to construct a theory of gender but rather, true to the ethnographic tradition, to use our materials to try to comprehend how gender operates in these streets. Our evidence suggests that the notion of gender as relational has some purchase. In fact, our material suggests that even Butler's own understanding of gender, where the "'being' of gender is an effect" (1999, 45)—that is, gender is constituted through performance—can still be understood in relational terms. For example, we worked with two married couples who each asked to be interviewed as a couple. Claire (in her thirties) and Max (in his forties) had just had their first baby. Claire hadn't worn jeans much when she was younger, as her parents disapproved of them (seeing them as "cheap"), and they had never been a fundamental part of her wardrobe; she first wore jeans when she was in her twenties. Max recalls being attracted to the fact that she wore skirts and more "feminine" clothing when they first met. This made her stand out. "She was very girly. In the early days I don't recall seeing her in trousers for months after we met. It just suited her, it's just part of her, it makes her stand out from the other girls with baggy jumpers and jeans." He seeks her advice when they go shopping together; as he jokes, "A man cannot be trusted on his own [when shopping]. You must have either your mom or your partner with you." In contrast to her clothing, he wears jeans regularly for work, and in a number of ways exemplifies the position of many men on the street in dressing to be "unseen." Their initial attraction came through mutual concern to maintain gender as difference, and this remains important to their relationship

The other couple we interviewed together, Eric and Margaret, were much older, in their seventies. It was Eric who got his first pair of jeans from a GI, discussed in chapter 1. Margaret has never really worn jeans, having been brought up in a time when most women wore skirts and were expected to be feminine. He, by contrast, has always worn jeans as casual attire. He still prefers to get dressed up when he goes out, as does she. Yet, in clear contrast to Claire and Max, whose simple conformity to gender as difference renders them quite conventional in the public sphere, Eric on occasion dresses to be "seen." His selection of ties and shirts (often clashing in patterns and colors) is intended to cultivate a look regarded as eccentric. For this it is important that he does not wear jeans, since jeans are exactly what his friends (also mostly in their seventies) will wear to the local pub. While his wife dresses up to go to church on Sundays, he will also, on the same day, dress conspicuously for the pub.

A third variation on the way the relationship within the couple interacts with wider relationships is found with Pauline and Tom, who were discussed in the previous chapter. They would be better described in terms of gender complementarity than gendered opposition. At no point does either talk about being attracted to or liking the other in terms of being "feminine" or "masculine." The only space in which gendered stereotypes are invoked is when Pauline talks about hating shopping with her female friends and being "the bloke." Nevertheless, she wants her daughter to be feminine, as expressed in the clothes that she buys for her; she talks of looking back at pictures of herself in dresses as a girl and thinking she looked pretty even though she has never enjoyed dressing in such a manner. Rather, it is in respect to her daughter that she says, "I want her to be able to express that girliness." Neither Tom nor Pauline spends a lot of time on appearance, and both seem to cultivate the idea of not being looked at or noticed. Although both of them have gone through a phase of wearing jeans, neither of them wears them anymore. Pauline often wears dark blue casual trousers, and Tom wears chinos and shirts in shades of brown and beige. This sense of a latent distinction, one that the parents never much expressed for themselves but which for that very reason may be more clearly projected onto their children, is common for mothers in London (Miller 1997). So while we started with a more simple image of teenagers rejecting identities projected onto them by their parents, we end with a much more complex sense of introjections and projections in which parents are often responding just as much to their memories of themselves at an earlier age, now vicariously expressed through their children.

CONCLUSION: GENDER, CONFORMITY, AND INDIVIDUALITY

This chapter has expanded upon the previous discussion of jeans as part of life stories by examining the place of jeans in relationships. The initial emphasis was on relationships within households based mainly on cases where we were able to work with several people within the same household. We later looked at relationships external to the household, including the formation of couples, which in turn leads to the creation of new households. Much of our evidence corresponds to the colloquial sense that children reach a point in which they may repudiate certain parental influences, turning more to peer groups and then to concerns with dating. In practice, however, all of these stages turn out to be both complex and varied.

Central to each stage in such a progression is the issue of gender. Gender was not something we necessarily sought to emphasize in our research, yet it soon became clear that parents often express their concerns and projections by ensuring that their children wear highly gendered clothing. In some households of South Asian origin this may take the form of simply refusing to let girls wear jeans, or of being worried about skinny jeans that go beyond emphasizing femininity to more overt displays of sexuality. By the same token, a common finding when talking to young women in these households is that they saw themselves as "tomboys," deemphasizing gender distinctions precisely to frustrate this projection of gender upon them by their parents. But gender conformity is by no means limited to parental control. It is as evident in the alternative movement toward peer groups of young teenagers who often cultivate stridently distinct gender stereotypes, especially when they start dating. It then continues within established couples, based on attraction through difference.

Jeans may become central to much of this negotiation around gender distinctions, partly because jeans themselves manage to both incorporate and refute gender as difference. For example, some of the women we worked with talked of wearing jeans all the time but adopted strategies to feminize them, either through some of the details embroidered onto the jeans or in the way they combined them within an outfit or accessorized them. Tracy, for example, wears jeans constantly, and she has a range of them. The position of jeans with her wardrobe is therefore dynamic, rather than always occupying the same position, such as "casual" clothing—for her they are able to transcend different types of clothing. Her husband also seems to live in jeans, which she refers to as his "old faithfuls." So in one respect this seems to mark their commonality. But there is a clear enough contrast between his "standard" style of male jeans and hers, one that becomes exaggerated when she combines her jeans with heels for a night out, or with an array of dressier tops.

So while denim may be worn by both men and women and can be thereby viewed as a unisex or genderless item, it is very rare for people to emphasize this possibility when they wear jeans to go out in. At the level of retail, jeans are usually are sold as "men's" and "women's" jeans, and even as "boyfriend" jeans. This last category is not really an androgynous look, as the woman is positioned in relationship to a man, albeit imaginary. This is extended in the choices evident in our field material, where women can also opt to wear tighter jeans with a higher proportion of elastane fibres. As is common in gender relations more generally, there is a sense that men's jeans remain masculine, often by being relatively unmarked. This reflects an ideal of the "ordinary bloke," while women's jeans are more often conspicuously gendered to accentuate their femininity. As John Berger (1972) wrote, "women appear"; they are the subjects of what Laura Mulvey (1975) discussed as the male gaze. Though clearly with peer groups girls are responding as much to other girls, it is possible to retain Mulvey's perspective by following more recent feminist writing such as that of Young (2005), who suggests that women internalize this sense of being the object of someone else's gaze, and that it affects how they see their own bodies.

Such discussions are echoed in many of our examples, where men commonly talk about their desire to be unseen or inconspicuous, while women dress up to go out. There are of course exceptions, as some women dress to be unseen, not only in their ordinary day clothing or casual wear but also when they are going out. Indeed, in the example of Eric and Margaret, the generalizations are reversed, as it is Eric rather than Margaret who wants to be conspicuous. Outside of such dressing to go out, we can see a more shared emphasis upon rather ordinary jeans, which tend to remain inconspicuous as everyday wear equally for both men and women. Though there may remain some differences between men's and women's jeans, these are not necessarily very evident.

Gender is not the only common theme. As is implied by the sequence of chapters in this book, which progress from the individual through relationships with other people and then to fashion, there is also a concern with the wider public sphere. When parents force their children to wear properly gendered clothing, this involves not just gender but also conformity and normativity more generally. The way an individual subsequently deals with gender may also play around with more individual or more conformist strategies. This is evident in the case of Joe and George, who manage to develop complementary styles of masculinity while avoiding what they might see as the "defensive" performative masculinity displayed by their landlord. Eric, on the other hand, uses an exaggerated sense of difference based on gender to become an eccentric figure, conspicuously individual when he goes to the pub. These issues of conformity and individuality are more fully developed in the next chapter, in relation to fashion.

CHAPTER 3

Fashion

The primary concern in this volume is with jeans as refracted through the experiences of the people who live in the three ordinary streets in North London where we carried out the research. We regard these individuals as the determinants of what jeans mean and how they come to matter. Our focus is upon their routines, their relationships, the broader trajectories of their lives, and the role that jeans have in these. But in a book about denim we cannot ignore the fact that jeans are also a commodity. The people who appear in this ethnography encounter jeans in the first instance as goods, most often in association with particular retail outlets or as particular brands. The companies that produce such brands work in competition and for profit and often have minor industries of their own devoted to the marketing and sales of jeans, trying to ensure positive associations between potential consumers and their particular labels.

We do not intend to deal directly with any of this commercial activity, yet it is still relevant as context, especially when we find evidence that a factor such as branding has come to be significant in the relationship between consumers and jeans. So even if the focus is on consumption, this needs to subsume whatever consequences can be observed of jeans' origins in commerce. There has been a huge proliferation of denim brands in recent years (Hang 2006), and in tandem, many chain stores have launched their own retail brands. As a result, it is almost impossible to go into a clothing store and not be able to buy a pair of jeans, in

Most paid for jeans	Total % of people
£0–15	7%
£16–25	15%
£26–50	43%
£51–90	18%
£91–120	3%
£121+	1%
No answer	12%

a seemingly vast array of styles and finishes. Jeans are available at all levels of the market, from £3 pairs to iconic brands such as Levi's and Diesel, which usually have their own shops as well as selling to other retail outlets, and the designer brands, which can sell at over £200 a pair. Although in our research we found there was a broad spectrum of what people were willing to pay for a pair of jeans, as the table above makes clear, only 1 percent of those who completed the questionnaire claimed to have ever paid more than £120. Far more common were the middle-range prices.

As well as a proliferation of prices and brands, there are now a wide range of styles of jeans available for purchase: boot cut, boyfriend, skinny, regular, high-waist, and low-rise, to name but a few. Most jeans are blue, though from the perspective of fashion, indigo blue jeans are an entirely different animal from light blue jeans. There is a much smaller and more fleeting market in jeans of various other colors, with black perhaps showing more staying power. There is an even greater range of effects and detailing that are critical not just to brand distinctions but also within brands, to create the brand range. An aspect of how brands articulate and create their difference is through their advertising. While this book is about what people wear, advertising is important as a context within which their clothing practices operate. It is worth noting here that there is a vast industry surrounding the advertising of jeans, and in some instances they draw upon concepts that we consider in this book, such as comfort, fit, or personalization. However, our discussion of these issues arises from the practices of wearing, rather than how these are advertised and branded. After all, it is at least as likely that people in advertising are picking up on what seems of interest to consumers as it is that consumers derive these concerns from the advertising. Thus in this chapter we will consider people's awareness of brands and advertising.

Within the shops there appears to be an extensive array of choice, so much so that marketers can argue that there now evidently exists a "right" pair of jeans for everybody, irrespective of taste or financial resources. This supposed situation of ultimate choice is, of course, illusory, given that in any one year particular styles dominate, at least if consumers want to remain in fashion. Skinny jeans, for example, have been popular for the last several years, and they are not at all a variety that anyone and everyone might feel comfortable wearing. What is more true is that behind this diversity there remains a kind of backbone of basic indigo blue jeans, with rivets, characteristic dual rows of stitching at the bottom, multiple pockets, some (but not too much) detailing, usually on the back pocket, and standard straightish legs. These remain dominant and constant, and in this case it really could be said that pretty much anyone and everyone can wear them in some form. These jeans have none of the temporalities and design input that we normally associate with the word *fashion,* yet one of the most common things we heard in our fieldwork was that such jeans always remain somehow "in fashion."

In this chapter, even if we are not concerned with the industry per se, we do need to examine how the people living on these streets deal with this apparent choice, starting with the anxieties of shopping for jeans and choosing the right style. Curiously, no one we interviewed talked of this range of denim styles as something positive. Rather, shopping for particular jeans commonly involved anxieties and traumas. The possibility that the perfect pair of jeans is out there seems to have added to the anxiety rather than alleviated it, as the burden is placed on the individual to find and buy them. After considering the process of shopping for jeans, we will then turn to the way the selection of jeans is linked to personal style. This may emerge from the way individuals associate themselves with a particular store brand, which in turn comes to express a certain continuity and consistency within their idea of a personal aesthetic.

Beyond the relationship to shopping and to particular brands there is the wider, and often more problematic and contradictory, relationship to fashion itself, and the perception of fashion as something external that changes and imposes its will upon people, including those who then feel threatened in their more constant relationship to the style of jeans with which they identify. Fashion may also be involved in the associations people create with particular typologies and categories of jeans, such as skinny and boot-cut. Other categories may emerge subsequently from those same associations, such as "old man" jeans. So the relationship to fashion is not just a way people deal with the commercial aspects of jeans. Perhaps rather more than with most clothing, this is also about how people create their own typologies of jeans within the wardrobe: a spectrum from which they choose jeans for particular occasions. This may be mapped onto styles offered in retail outlets, but it also may be very different, as types of jeans are linked to particular events or degrees of smartness.

SHOPPING

None of those who took part in this study seemed to regard shopping for jeans as either an especially enjoyable leisure pursuit or something easy. At best they thought of it as simply part and parcel of the general burden of shopping for clothing that one needs. This is opposed to holiday shopping or buying clothes one doesn't need, which generally are viewed as pleasurable activities, but these are less likely to include jeans. Those who tend to regard jeans purchasing as just another form of shopping tend to be males and especially older males. They may not positively identify with shopping but don't regard buying jeans as anything particularly special or especially problematic. It's just a chore to go out and buy what is most commonly an "ordinary" pair of jeans. At the other end of the spectrum are young women, especially teenagers, for whom shopping for clothes is often an anxiety-producing experience, but when it involves jeans it might be regarded as particularly traumatic. For this group, shopping is often a predominant leisure activity, associated with sociability (done with friends) and pleasure, yet at the same time the hunt for jeans in particular is seen as difficult.

For this group the two key problems appeared to be the variety of jeans they had to choose from and the problem of getting jeans that would fit. For a teenager such as Ches, jeans buying is much harder than anything else: "Tracksuits and so on, once they're your size they will fit, but because there are so many different types of jeans you have to try them on." For her, consumer choice is not an array of wonderful possibilities. Rather, she conveys her sense of despondency when she says that after trying to cope with all the "hassle" of jeans shopping she finds she simply can't be bothered and might in the end "just pick up my size and hope for the best." She talks about the complexities of how jeans (and trousers more widely) fail to fit, not like a top, which is "easy." In trousers there are "length and thighs, waist." This applies not just to females. The Australian Joe talked about how he had tried on a pair of jeans in the fitting room and initially liked they way they fit. But after he had been wearing them for a while they began to feel "too restricting . . . around the thigh." As a result of this experience, he would now always "test them and go for a walk around the shop . . . because in the fitting rooms you can try them on" but cannot move around.

Another teenage girl, Ivana, originally from Kosovo, reinforced the difficulties of shopping for jeans, but contrasts with Ches in that she always knows exactly what she is looking for: "low-rise" and "dark blue." She usually buys in the chain store Oasis, not because the shop "means anything to her" but because she happened to have found a pair of jeans from that shop that were particularly "comfortable." Even though Ivana has come to know Oasis pretty well and is aware of her own color and style preferences, she still finds it "hard to find one pair that fit really well." She was recently frustrated by the fact that "skinny ones were in fashion and I couldn't find the normal cut that I wanted." This exemplifies the general point that most people like to stick to a particular style or type once they have found "their" jeans, and are then frustrated when changes in fashion populate the stores with quite other styles of jeans, creating pressure to buy different jeans every couple of years. We have other stories of people finding something close to those "ideal jeans," only to find the next time around that the shop has stopped stocking them. Generally such jeans are regarded as ideal because of their fit to the individual, which is not necessarily seen as connected to either brand or their relationship to fashion. This is precisely the problem for those seeking to repeat an initial purchase, because it is brand and fashion that the shops focus on.

This is reinforced by the difficulty people have with this practice of fit. The other Australian, George, is in his own words "freakishly tall" (he is six foot six) and very slim. He is limited to shops that stock such sizes and still has to wear them low-slung in order for them to reach the floor. Nneka, originally from Sierra Leone, buys most of her jeans when on trips to the United States, where she claims she can find a better fit for black women's bodies. She says she struggles to find ones in UK shops that fit properly on the bottom. Others avoid shopping for jeans by having them handed down by relatives, especially one woman whose sister is single and spends a lot of money on jeans, which she either gets tired of or which crowd out other items in her wardrobe, at which point she hands them on.

FASHION AND BRANDS

For the reasons just outlined, it is easier for a consumer who is prepared to move beyond the fit of a particular pair of jeans and acquiesce in an association instead with either a particular shop or brand. This can develop into a long-term association, with even a sense of "loyalty" to that brand (Fournier 1998). So we might expect them to develop a relationship to fashion and branding as promoted by commerce. The idea that fashion in a broader sense becomes part of what people are used to wearing over a period of their life was explored in chapter 1 through life histories. People saw their own lives in terms of styles of clothing that were current over particular periods of time. The term *fashion* often meant not the narrower drive of commerce trying to influence the clothes of a particular season but broader cultural trends that related to decades or even generations, with which people do identify. In a similar vein, most people on these streets were largely unaware of the vast majority of more transient brands, and did not differentiate in any detail particular brands within this spectrum of choice. Part of the questionnaire asked them to name brands they were familiar with, and most participants struggled to go beyond three brands, either then or later in more detailed conversations. In fact, they were generally unaware of the advertising campaigns or connotations of many of the brands that they do wear. So even if advertising campaigns use the concepts we discuss in the following chapters, such as comfort, it is more likely that they have done their research and are trying to follow consumers' concerns. There is no evidence that advertising is the actual source of such concerns, since there is no evidence that it impinges upon shoppers at all aside from a couple of historically iconic campaigns, such as for Levi's.

The ways in which advertising taps into, and draws upon, what people do anyway is exemplified in the case of boyfriend jeans. In our research we didn't encounter anyone who actually wore a boyfriend's jeans, yet several wore readymade "boyfriend jeans," a jeans style present in retail outlets. In previous research, Woodward (2011) found several women who did actually wear their boyfriend's jeans, whether as a means of extending their wardrobe, or feeling the security of a partner's love, or mediating the partner's absence. In this case it seemed clear that consumers' practice had been copied to become a commercial category, rather than being the other way round. A similar phenomenon is seen in the case of "distressing" denim, where again it is commerce that follows the lead given by consumers' transformation of their jeans. As a commercial enterprise, fashion, with its mechanisms of branding and advertising, operates through promoting change. Yet what jeans exemplify, for many people we interviewed, is continuity, as people want to continue buying and wearing a particular style of jeans. Simply because skinny jeans or high-waisted jeans are presented as fashionable or attractive does not mean that people will wear them; that depends much more upon long-term material practices and also what is already in people's wardrobes (Woodward 2009).

For many people, too, there was a clear disavowal of fashion as something they claimed to have no interest in whatsoever. In some cases this verbal disavowal was echoed in practice, in the absence of fashionable clothing. Yet there could also be evident contradictions, as for example with one such woman who professes to have no interest in what is in fashion while wearing white skinny jeans and a tunic top in the precise style of the moment. One reason for such contradictions may be that acknowledging the impact of fashion has the effect of lowering the credit given to one's own agency or choice. Also, there can be a genuine lack of choice, so buying whatever is in the shops at the time has the effect of placing the shopper in fashion whether he or she feels positive about this or not. And people may indirectly follow fashion merely by conforming to their peers.

What came across as a common pattern was that many people find it much easier to express strong feelings about what they don't like and won't wear than to articulate what they do like (Wilk 1997). Maria, originally from Portugal, claims she has no interest in clothes at all, and when she was younger she wore whatever her mother bought her. However, once she starts to go into more detail about the role of clothing in her life, she comes up with a very elaborated set of ideas around what she will and won't wear. Those who expressed positive interest in brands and fashion tended to be the younger participants. But the complication there was that they often had little by way of income; as one eighteen-year-old woman put it, she and her friends are not into brands "since Primark came along."* A typical woman in her late teens, she possesses a pair of Levi's jeans but doesn't much like them, as they don't fit well. She is more devoted to an £8 pair from Primark that are "quite nice." The only person in these three streets who could be said to have

---

* Primark is a particularly low-cost and highly successful clothing store. In a previous study Burikova and Miller (2010) found that some au pairs, who had very little income, saw the geography of London mainly in terms of travel between branches of Primark.

very extensive knowledge about jeans as fashion was someone who had previously worked in the denim industry and was also given to wearing expensive designer jeans.

It was not even that people were familiar with brands but then didn't wear them. More commonly, we found, people wore brands that they knew nothing much about. Even where we did find people who profess an interest in and fondness for branded jeans, they tended in practice to focus upon only a small part of the actual spectrum of brands available. An exception might be David, whom we first introduced in chapter 1. He has a brother who is five years older who lives and works in Hong Kong. This brother has been handing down jeans to David since he was at university, stimulating David's interest in labels such as Evisu and Versace even though he was unable to afford them (when he was buying them himself, he generally had to buy less expensive labels such as French Connection). This is significant since many people who had relatives abroad were aware that brands were both more important and better known to those living in other countries as compared to those living in the United Kingdom. People might expect that designer jeans would be of "better quality" or that a Levi's shop would be a good place to start one's search, as the clerks in that store "have more knowledge" about jeans. Yet in practice a label was more commonly a post hoc justification for buying something one had chosen on other grounds.

Even those who, like David, had obtained designer jeans as gifts or hand-me-downs didn't necessarily thereby develop a positive relationship with them. More typical was Jo, a woman in her early twenties who had a pair of DVB jeans, designed by Victoria Beckham, which retail at over £200, given to her by a friend. She has had them for three or four years but has no particular attachment to or interest in them; she says they are "quite comfy" but not particularly better quality than the ones she usually wears, and she seems not at all interested in the fact that they were designed by a celebrity. Most people we interviewed have no particular loyalty to a brand because of its associations; rather, the relationship is cultivated over time through the practices of wearing. The woman with the DVB jeans says they are not "worth the money. Jeans are just jeans at the end of the day." When she talks about the difference between designer jeans and non-designer jeans, she says, "If you were to blindfold me and stick a pair of jeans on, I wouldn't be able to tell." The real gift is not the celebrity label but the fact that someone else did the shopping for her, since she professes to "absolutely hate shopping." Although this is not something people are explicit about, it is quite likely that in London a dismissal of brands is almost seen as a mark of intelligence or maturity, of not being "taken in" by commerce in general or fashion in particular. Brands are often assumed to appeal more to teenagers, who are easier to dupe. This is part of how Londoners create their particular sense of sophistication and would be consistent with other research we have conducted in the past on clothes shopping (Clarke and Miller 2002; Woodward 2007).

It is not, however, that people have looked past fashion and branding to some more authentic or craftlike knowledge of jeans themselves. People are equally ignorant of and disinterested in the constituent parts of jeans. Other than perhaps an awareness of some jeans having stretch or some sense of the broad style of a pair of jeans, people knew very little about the cut of the jeans or the materiality of denim. Virtually no one among our participants had any particular knowledge about or interest in cotton, indigo, or rivets, or in how jeans are manufactured or dyed, by whom, and where. As with so many shop-bought goods, the point of purchase is the beginning of their relationship to the product; its prior history or what goes into its production is simply not considered. When expressly asked, some people suggest they might favor fair trade or organic goods, but in clothing, unlike food, this is not something that the kind of people who live in these streets have yet developed any active consciousness of. Furthermore, none of the people we interviewed have customized their jeans or talk of mending them to any great extent. This mirrors wider trends, where few people mend their clothing (beyond basic sewing on of buttons) or make their own, due to a combination of loss of sewing skills and also the convenience of cheap clothing in the shops.

It may then at first appear paradoxical in the light of all that has just been said that a number of people do have an absolute devotion and loyalty to one brand or shop, especially as these people tend to be those who have the least general interest in brands as such, that is, middle-aged or older men. Yet they often expressed the clearest passion for a particular brand, which in most cases meant Levi's. In several cases it was wives or mothers who talked about the way their husbands or sons only ever wore Levi's—they worked, breathed, and slept in them. This affection for Levi's was probably the single most passionate resonance between individuals and their jeans that we encountered. But this does not really contradict our earlier arguments, since it is clear that the advantage of this singular attachment is largely that it solves the problem of otherwise having to bother with even thinking about alternative brands, or shopping more generally. It made the purchase of jeans extremely straightforward. For others, an association with Marks & Spencer or Next worked equally well as an avoidance of alternatives.

If we look for the reason that Levi's are most often the brand involved in this particular passion, we might assume that it goes back to the various associations that jeans had in the past with cool cowboys, with America, or with sexiness. It is probable that this was originally the case. But most of those who currently have a relationship to Levi's and similar jeans do not seem drawn to these more historical points of reference. Rather more important is what could be called the "Jeremy Clarkson effect." Clarkson, the presenter of *Top Gear*, a television program devoted to cars, was notorious for some years because he always wore the same style of stonewashed tight jeans and also sported the fashion faux pas of double denim (that is, blue jeans and a denim jacket). Several people we interviewed know that there is a popular perception that jeans became very unpopular in the 1990s because they were associated with unfashionable older males such as Clarkson, and one of our informants confirms that in his late thirties he stopped wearing blue jeans and a denim jacket because he was worried he would look like he was having a "midlife crisis." This association with the unfashionable middle-aged men is one that runs counter to attempts of advertising campaigns, which tend to focus specifically upon attracting the young and the fashionable, and rarely the types of people who actually wear a brand or type of jeans (although with some long-established brands advertising may promote notions of authenticity or consistency).

What is less remarked upon and perhaps more important for our study was the positive association created by the Jeremy Clarkson effect. Though they are not the kind of consumers that advertisers usually try to attract, unfashionable middle-aged men are actually a significant market of people who routinely wear jeans and also have strong brand loyalty. Although Tom, for example, no longer wears jeans, he says he went through a period of almost twenty years wearing first exclusively Levi's and then exclusively Wrangler. He says he had a sense that he could trust such jeans—that he did not need to worry about what to wear or about being fashionable or unfashionable. He could just be an "ordinary bloke" in them. At least with something such as Levi's 501s the consumer really can develop a more personal relationship, such that once a pair of jeans is worn out one can go back to the same shop and buy the same style again, repeating that relationship.

TYPOLOGIES OF JEANS

Levi's speak to the predilections of middle-aged men who cling to the same style of jeans. But this group is clearly only a small proportion of the people we worked with. While there were others who also swear by a single style of jeans (which they often regard as "classic" or "ordinary"), many more of those we interviewed had developed their own typology of jeans, which may or may not have any resonance with commercial typologies. These may incorporate different colors (usually just blue and black, however), levels of wear or distressing, and cut (such as boot cut, skinny, classic, or boyfriend). In a few cases the organization of the wardrobe reflects that found in shops, which may then assist in subsequent shopping because they can easily identify gaps that need to be filled, which for them may correspond with different situations in their lives. In practice they see a gradation of jeans that is also a measure of smartness and suitability for different occasions. For all but a few, brand is absent from this wardrobe organization. Although many people we interviewed possessed enough jeans to differentiate them, this does not necessarily signify an active accumulation of a range, since people tend to keep jeans for long periods, including some they rarely wear; rather, this may reflect the way available jeans have changed over time. As the table on the following page demonstrates, the majority of people we interviewed own between one and five pairs of jeans.

If people do not necessarily repeat commercial categories, it gives them freedom to be creative about their own. Jo, the woman who has the hand-me-down DVB jeans and who doesn't care much about clothing, is not the kind of person to organize her wardrobe by brands. She does, however, have a clear typology of jeans; she is someone who wears jeans all the time when she is not at work. Almost all participants had a wardrobe typology, organizing their clothes by the different domains of their lives; for some people, jeans are present in every domain, while for others they may be an entirely separate domain. Jo has five pairs and wears "normal" jeans on weekends, when she dresses casually and wears trainers with them. She pairs her smarter skinny jeans with boots, and also wears them in winter with her Ugg boots. To go out she may put on her black jeans, accompanied by a dressier top.

Skinny jeans are a style that has effectively replaced boot-cut jeans (previously touted as the most flattering for most women's body shapes) in many people's wardrobes. But skinnies pose particular problems, as they can be incredibly tight. For this reason some women talk of never

Number of jeans owned	Total % of people
0	9%
1–5	55%
6–10	22%
11–15	6%
16–20	1%
21+	1%
No answer	4%

leaving boot-cuts, as skinnies don't suit them, whereas others talk of wanting to wear them even if they "don't have the thighs for them." For most women this has also involved an adaptation of the wardrobe, with longer tunic-style tops becoming popular as a cover-up for jeans that may be too tight. Jo sees skinnies as smarter jeans, which means that for her they preclude wearing trainers. For others such as Ches, skinny jeans can be casual when matched with flat ballet pumps. In effect, the wardrobe becomes the transition point between a concern with purchase and a concern with wearing. A shift in fashion has effectively dictated a change from boot-cut to skinny, but this is then domesticated by rendering skinny jeans into a series of alternative looks through the way they are matched with shoes and tops. Finally, this allows a change in fashion to be made subservient to wearers' requirements for jeans that match the different situations they go out in.

That this can be as true for men as for women is illustrated by Arvind, who has gradually constructed a wardrobe suited both to how he feels and to the occasions for which he must dress. Born in Uganda to a Gujerati family who moved to England soon afterward, he has lived in this area of North London since 1985, currently with his wife, their two children, and his parents. He has been wearing jeans since he was in sixth form (that is, about sixteen years of age), although his parents never wore jeans and his sister did only rarely, as jeans were deemed insufficiently feminine. He always wore "standard" jeans as a teenager, but as he got into hip-hop music, he started to adopt a baggier style. He wore jeans every day in sixth form (for him, as for others, jeans pretty much took on the role of the now absent school uniform), and this continued at university, as they were the "easiest" item of clothing. When he first started working as a retail manager, he moved to only wearing jeans at the weekend. Finally, jeans were displaced by tracksuits as the ideal garment to relax into when he returns home from work.

A tracksuit is also what Arvind's wife wears at home, as she was brought up in Bombay never wearing jeans and moved to the United Kingdom when she was twenty-three. She still doesn't wear jeans at home as a sign of respect to his parents, who now live with them; nor does Arvind. Instead they wear jeans for casual events outside the house—to "pop into the shops" or to go to soccer matches. Yet Arvind always wears jeans to smarter occasions as well. He has five or six pairs of jeans, including one pair each of Levi's 501s, Pepes, and Armani jeans (these last are black and for special occasions). The others are "standard"—for example, a pair of George jeans from the supermarket chain Asda (a subsidiary of Walmart). Arvind takes more care of the designer jeans and leaves them on hangers, rather than folded with the other jeans. He has two pairs of distressed jeans (the Pepes and a George pair), two black pairs, and one light blue pair; the rest are indigo blue. While this creates a range of colors, levels of smartness, and labels, the basic style is the same for them all: straight-leg. So Arvind exploits some parameters of difference but not others. While for some people we interviewed jeans are strictly casual wear, in Arvind's wardrobe jeans cross many different domains, so he can wear them to a wide range of social occasions; this has allowed them to become a dominant form of clothing for him. Of all his jeans, he wears the Levi's the most; his wife appreciates the Armanis as the smarter pair that are appropriate for "special occasions, birthday parties, and barbeques." He would wear these with proper shoes, while trainers are fine for all the other jeans. He also has a tailored black jacket that he would wear with the Armani jeans for a milestone birthday or similar event.

There are many people on the street who would serve as variants on this theme explored here through Jo and Arvind, the main distinction between them being that Jo has to adapt her wardrobe to shifts in the underlying fashion regime of jeans, while Arvind seems more free to construct a typology largely of his own making that is finely attuned to the requirements imposed by the occasions he wear jeans for and the sensibilities of those around him.

SPECIFICITY AND THE GOLDILOCKS PHENOMENON

As is already evident from the previous discussions in this chapter, there are a number of ways in which people seem to have created a particular relationship to jeans that by no means simply follows the way in which jeans are created in standard categories or indeed understood by the commercial forces that originally create them. Whether in reference to middle-aged men who wear a single variety of jeans or people such as Jo for whom a range of jeans can be worn on various occasions, individuals seem to frequently develop quite a strong sense of which jeans are "right" for them, which mirrors Woodward's (2007) discussion of the sense of "this is me" in women's clothing. This doesn't necessary correspond to some nuance of style or denim finish, as would be understood by the industry. It is rather a characterization of what people feel are the parameters within which a pair of jeans can be recognized as "their" type of jeans. As already noted, often this can be more eloquently expressed in terms of the kind of jeans people really don't like or "wouldn't be seen dead in" than in any clear description of what it is they are looking for in jeans.

For example, a man who wore only black jeans as a teenager now only has dark indigo straight-leg jeans; as he says, "That's jeans to me . . . real jeans." Authenticity is a key idea that is deployed in advertising for jeans, although it tends to relates to heritage and associations of Americana rather than the sense in which this man deploys the term *real*. (For a discussion of authenticity in relation to the type of denim used and how it is made, see Keet 2011.) Although he has many pairs of jeans from a range of brands, such as Armani and Yves Saint Laurent, he has only this one jeans type, since all companies that make jeans will include in their range such standard styles. He only wears them as casual attire because he can't bring himself to wear jeans with shoes, only with trainers, as they otherwise just "feel wrong" to him. He is very particular about fit: when he was in Dubai he found a pair of jeans that "was the perfect waist fitting" and "perfect everywhere else" apart from them being too long; because "I don't like my jeans hanging down and dragging across and I don't like to turn them up," he had them tailored. He was the sole example in our study of someone who had his jeans tailored, but he exemplifies the more general concern that people need to get jeans that are right for them.

The logic that lies behind this often strong concern to get jeans "just right" corresponds to what we might call the "Goldilocks phenomenon." For example, Sharon, who is married and has two daughters, has lived on the street since 1981. She is not someone who cares a great deal about her appearance, nor is her husband. She started to wear jeans in her early twenties, as "everyone was." More particularly, her brother was the "trendsetter" and she was the "follower." Her jeans would generally be regarded as "conservative" rather than fashionable. Similarly, she prefers jeans that appear neither brand-new nor too worn, but rather are "middle-of-the-road." The jeans she wears and has always worn are "classical fit, neither tight nor flare," even if she now wears ones that are slightly lower-slung. The term she employs, "classical fit," is similar to one that is used in the fashion industry. "Classic fit" jeans are seen as the archetype from which other styles develop; common features are a straight leg and greater ease at the bottom. However, while this classification may often be used as shorthand to indicate a certain type of fit, it is not necessarily informative for the customer. That is, "classic fit" is not necessarily the same in each shop. Nonetheless, it is a term that has purchase among consumers, as our material demonstrates, and it is one that is utilized by retailers, albeit in different ways.

There is strong sense of balance in what Sharon wears. She is quite particular, but what she is being particular about is the need to position what she wears in the middle of some spectrum of difference. She has three pairs of jeans, two of which are identical: midlevel classic-style blue denim. The third pair is cream-colored and she views them as dressier. In many ways the style is very plain, but she says that when she bought them "I did have quite a job. Some were too flared. I looked at all different types. I think in the end I must have tried twelve pairs. I thought that if I want to buy new jeans I want them to be right." Perhaps the best way to understand the Goldilocks phenomenon is to say that many people are keen to buy jeans they regard as "classic," "standard," or just "normal"—that is, "just right." This creates a very strong sense of specificity in what might otherwise seem to be very straightforward "regular" jeans. Ches too has a Goldilocks element to her selections, in her case involving the ideal of fit in relation to the body: "Baggy jeans can make you look a bit fat, but skinny jeans can also make you look a bit fat. There has to be a medium."

All of this can become something of a struggle, as illustrated by Ivana. She has five pairs of jeans, including a skinny black pair and three pairs of blue jeans that are just normal. She sees black jeans as requiring slightly more consideration, whereas the blue ones are "easier to wear—they're just normal." So, like many other people, her wardrobe contains some jeans differentiation, but not an especially elaborate or radical range of styles. She is also someone who characterizes herself as "restrained" and "not very emotional." She doesn't want to wear exuberant clothes that would stand out or make her be noticed. But for most women (though less so for men), owning only one type of jeans would not achieve this effect of normality, of not standing out, simply because different occasions require different looks. Within each context there will be something that works as the unnoticed "normal" look. One can stand out by refusing to dress for a special occasion, for example. It is the consistency with which Ivana strives for such impersonality that paradoxically could be regarded as her personal style.

CONCLUSION

This first part of the book has provided the general background to our study, outlining and analyzing much of the evidence from our interviews. The next section will start to focus much more narrowly on the particular aspect of jeans that seemed to us most significant and which takes us on a path toward our later theoretical discussion of the art of the ordinary. Already there are some clear conclusions that are important, not just because of what they say about people's relationship to jeans and our subsequent focus upon the ordinary but also because of the way the study of jeans seems to contradict so much that is commonly assumed about people's relationship to clothing and to fashion more generally, in particular in relationship to change. For example, one of these common assumptions is that fashion is now "fast" and constantly changing (Reinach 2005; for a critique of this, see Woodward 2009), or that fashion is predicated upon changes that are either "top-down" (Veblen 1899; Simmel 1957) or driven by creativity as a "bottom-up" process (Hebdige 1979). Our denim ethnography challenges these notions of constant change and many other rather glib statements about fashion, such as the idea that people require constant innovation or a sense that they are rejecting a mainstream. Some do, some of the time, but what they mainly wear is denim.

In this chapter we addressed the world of commerce and fashion within which jeans are produced. But what we found is that the attention to commerce has to be muted, because on the streets people pay much less regard to either commerce or fashion than might have been anticipated. There is an extraordinary discrepancy between the world of fashion and clothing that is portrayed by journalism and the media, and indeed by the commercial forces that create clothing, and the way ordinary people actually relate to that same clothing. It is not that people have no regard for fashion; it is rather that in practice fashion means something very different for them. More work on production and commerce can be found in our Global Denim Project (e.g., Chakravarti 2011; Comstock 2011; Keet 2011; Pinheiro 2011; Wilkinson-Weber 2011).

It is clear that the dynamics of style in clothing are very significant in the lives of most people. It seems quite natural to our participants to narrate their entire life trajectory in terms of a changing background of styles in which clothing and associated trends in music are the key components of any given period of time. Whether expressed as the style of a particular generation or that of a given decade, the detail comes from what people in general wore during that period. These same informants seemed equally comfortable assessing the degree to which they saw themselves as either conforming to or absenting themselves from that dominant trend.

As long as fashion refers to these broader cultural shifts, many people associate themselves and others with fashion. But when the term is used more narrowly, as is generally the case within the media, to refer only to the transient trends of one specific season or brand, then most people (with the exception of teenagers), despite reading countless magazines and newspapers and listening to endless programs that discuss fashion, seem to feel quite distant from these imperatives, even resenting and actively dissociating themselves from what they regard as a commercially driven pressure on their lives. In a similar manner, most people have very limited interest in branding. For some people a single brand, such as Levi's, will work well enough to stand for branding in general, while for others Primark has now come to stand for the desire to get inexpensive, good-value garments in lieu of an interest in brands.

One could conclude that the money and effort that have been put into fashion marketing have resulted in a general sense of alienation and distance between most people and the fashion industry. Jeans express this with perhaps greater clarity than most garments. There are those people, especially young women, who try to follow fashion jeans and contend with the plethora of types and brands, but as a result they find shopping for jeans a horrendous experience, with an oppressive pressure to find the perfect jeans. Most people instead look for jeans on an entirely different basis, ignoring brands and fashion dictates; they seek a pair that fits them personally and that thereby asserts their individuality as a body against the generics of fashion and branding. Having done the requisite research and finally located the exact pair of jeans that works for them, they may be unable to capitalize on that effort next time around, since those jeans often are no longer available and they have to start all over again. This can make them resentful toward the fashion industry. The highly complex nature of fit, determined against retailer criteria during garment development and then subsequently judged by the wearer, is a difficult foundation for providing garments to large populations. Without a common understanding of "fit" and the fact that so few of the population have had a garment made to fit them, the retailer and customer are engaged in a cat-and-mouse routine to satisfy and find satisfaction in clothing in terms of fit. Finding well-fitted garments becomes a trial, complicated by changing retailer offerings and the changing nature of people's bodies and perceptions.

This ambivalent attitude toward fashion is not that important to most people, at least compared to the ambivalence they feel with regard to other influences on how they dress. The far more significant tension is likely to be between an individual and his or her parents or peer group, or more generally whether an individual wants to stand out or appear unmarked in relation to those around him or her. While in our research we dutifully inquired about people's consideration of jeans as brands and fashion, it is clear that the relationship to clothes we have documented in this chapter is in essence mainly an instrument in people's relationship to others and to the their personal life history.

This discrepancy became evident only because we chose to study clothing through a more ethnographic perspective, which allowed us to understand what aspects of clothing matter to people, in terms of both what they say and what emerges from our observation of their practice. The problem with the vast literature on clothing and fashion is that it is so focused upon haute couture, designers, and the industry (for example, Vinken 2005; Koda and Bolton 2005; Tungate 2005) that it generates accepted ideas about what matters to people. This literature is not subject to the audit of scholarship that might contradict its assertions about what fashion is and how it matters. For us, distancing ourselves from this literature helped clear away a substantial amount of the debris strewn on the path to understanding just how significant and even profound jeans have become to ordinary people today—and the significance of the term *ordinary*.

The content of this chapter provides a bridging point between the previous chapters and those that follow, as we now propose to turn from the negative point of consumers' disregard for fashion to our more positive findings. If it is clear that most people are relatively indifferent to knowledge about how jeans are made or where, and indifferent to many of the blandishments of marketing, then there is something else going on that they are not in the least indifferent to. This chapter shows that people seem very concerned to get jeans "right." Most seem to have quite specific ideas about which jeans are right for them. This precision may concern color and style or a range of factors combined, but it is mainly explicated in vague terms such as *comfort* and *fit*. Yet this can amount to quite a personal relationship to jeans. This is easiest to see when we are dealing with a middle-aged man who never wears anything other than Levi 501s, and harder when people say they simply "know" what they are looking for (which is largely a match to something they have already worn). We are not trying to suggest that people never want to change their jeans or are impervious to fashion. Commonly they also possess items that are more fashionable and of the moment, but these may not be the jeans that they seem most concerned about. The paradox within this chapter is that people become anxious and distressed when shopping for jeans that are commonly described as anything but special. And even when there is a variety of jeans available, some for everyday wear, some for dressing up, within each category consumers look for what they regard as "classic" or "regular" version of these categories. They may buy an example of some new trend such as skinnies but then hardly ever wear them. Often when they do respond to media representations, these involve anti-fashion styles (such as "old man" jeans) or jeans that commerce produces to replicate consumers' practice (such as boyfriend jeans or distressed jeans).

It is perhaps no great surprise that jeans have a particularly ambiguous relationship to fashion. Jeans represent a form of clothing whose core style has remained relatively unchanged since its invention by Levi Strauss, and we might have expected that this lack of change would make it easier to buy jeans than to buy other clothing. However, it seems that while jeans are seen as very standard and ordinary, people struggle to get this sense of standard and ordinary right. This suggests there is something quite significant at stake in the ability of jeans to exemplify this state of being ordinary. Even though these are "just jeans," people are still very precise about what they won't wear, and will work hard to find the ones they are actually comfortable being associated with. This is our point of departure for the next three chapters, which take us from the more general ethnography of jeans wearing to focus more closely on these issues of "being comfortable" and "becoming ordinary" and investigates what it is that is at stake in this struggle to embody ordinariness.

CHAPTER 4

Comfortable

PRACTICAL COMFORT

Despite the wide range of people we interviewed for this project, one thing we heard over and over was that what matters most to individuals about their jeans is simply that they are "comfortable." While this may seem dismissive of most of the factors that we have been discussing so far, on closer interrogation this seemingly straightforward word, *comfortable,* can be seen to be both complex and profoundly important. Comfort is far more than just the feel of a fabric, as this physical experience also encodes a sense of what seems suitable or appropriate for a particular person. More than this, we will consider the ways in which what comes to appear "natural" is in fact far from it. We need to explore the process that is called, in the social sciences, naturalization— the process by which something that otherwise might seem arbitrary comes to appear natural, obvious, or commonsensical.

In our research interviews the term *comfortable* soon established itself as the basic legitimation for why one might wear jeans. People constantly came back to this term as a means to explain why they liked particular jeans. They might suggest that they preferred to wear Levi's because "I found them comfortable" or "they were a comfortable fit." Both terms (*fit* and *comfort*) are very personal to the individual and may not accord with the criteria used in the commercial creation of the garment. During garment development similar questions about fit and comfort will have been asked, but the factors are more controlled by what manufacturers can change, while for consumers it is more a matter of accommodation, since they have to live with garments that are already made, and attempt to find one that works with their sense of what fits well and is comfortable.

For our informants, it seemed that comfort was viewed as giving reasonable and sufficient grounds for determining what one might wear. When people expand on the term, it soon becomes clear that this seems like a reasonable explanation because for them comfort indicates a physical relationship between an item of clothing and the body. Comfort is presented as being about how someone feels, which is assumed to simply follow from the qualities of the garment. This in turn relates to the wider environment. Often comfort is expressed in the avoidance of the negative experience of feeling uncomfortable. This is commonly aligned to that ubiquitous British topic, the weather. For example, many people said of jeans, "Just not in the summer," or "When it's hot I don't wear jeans."

The vast majority of women find denim to be unsuitable for hot weather, as the fabric is seen as thick and potentially stifling. In particular, women talk about wearing skirts more often in summer than in winter because of the heat and the sensation of freeing their legs from being enclosed. But , as one of the above quotations demonstrates, there were also some, albeit not many, people who felt exactly the opposite and saw jeans as better suited to hot weather. Some who had experience of or originally came from warmer climates often suggested that jeans were entirely unsuited to the hot weather of, say, Australia or Turkey, but then also noted that people in tropical countries seemed to wear jeans more often than people in the United Kingdom. So the logic of comfort doesn't seem to entirely dictate what people actually do.

In practice most people seem to wear jeans at least occasionally all year round. A similar situation holds with regard to rain. The majority of participants feel that it's obvious that jeans are less suited to rainy weather, in that they soak up the water and take longer to dry than other garments. "In rain jeans are definitely the worst. They get cold and wet and they take ages to dry. I hate it." But a few suggest that denim is better at protecting them from the rain. Certainly most informants feel that wearing denim is suited to their current situation in London even though they simultaneously see the United Kingdom as particularly susceptible to wet weather. There can be more subtleties and distinctions— for example, one person thinks baggy jeans are unsuitable for rain but that skinny jeans are okay because they are less likely to trail on the floor and get wet in puddles.

Although there are relationships between the properties of the fabric and how it responds to water or how hot or cold the body beneath becomes, these properties alone do not determine or explain the reasons people give for liking or wearing their jeans. For example, both people who argue that jeans are good in the rain and those who think they are bad in the rain use the same arguments of comfort and practicality. These are asserted as a kind of common sense, irrefutable since they are based on the physical properties of the textile. It is assumed that "no one in their right mind" would want to wear something that kept them wet or were oppressively hot. Similar arguments are made with regard to the suitability of jeans for particular occupations or activities. For example, some people say that jeans are best for dirty work or work that involves physical labor: "I find them comfortable, and for the work we do they're awfully practical. They are practical for mealtime supervisors. If you get dirty, they're easy to maintain." Says another, "They are hard-wearing, you don't have to wash them often! [Laughs] They're just comfortable jeans, aren't they? There just a comfortable pair of clothes to put on." But another participant explains, "They can be uncomfortable at times, because if you're sitting on a train or something for a long time, they do get quite sticky." There doesn't need to be consistency here. The same man who says that jeans can be uncomfortable recognizes that his wife prefers jeans—she "has got a thing about wearing it when she travels." This proximity of the opposite arguments means he has to demote his account from a universal to a mere personal preference: "I don't know, I find it uncomfortable to travel in denim."

On closer inspection, the idea of a practical relationship to some functional property of jeans may take one of two contradictory forms. Sometimes what is implied is not that jeans are comfortable because they are more finely tailored or engineered to the wearer's precise body shape, but rather that people are more relaxed about the look of jeans on the body, so it matters less how precisely they fit, which in turn makes them comfortable. The alternative refers back to the concept of "fit" discussed in the last chapter, in which to be fully comfortable one needs to find jeans that precisely match the wearer's particular physique, with the ideal being bespoke jeans.

The next stage in this logic of comfort goes from practical comfort in terms of the body to practical ease in terms of jeans being relatively low-maintenance compared to any other kind of garment: "I found and do find jeans very comfortable. And so practical. So easy to maintain. If you wash them and put them in the dryer sometimes there's no need to press them. If you've left them long in the dryer, then they may need it. But you can get away with not ironing them, and I certainly do." Jeans are relatively low-maintenance because people's regimes of clothing care are different for jeans than for most other garments (Shove 2003; Fletcher 2008). It was very common to hear that people wash their jeans significantly less often than any other clothing, even when they wear them more often. This is all relative. Some participants who wash all other items of clothing every time they wear them make an exception for jeans, which they say they can wear two or three times before washing. Others who wash clothes every week or so will leave jeans to be washed every three weeks or so. The reasons put forward for this vary. As one participant put it, "They hold the dirt more." There is not the same expectation that jeans will look as immaculate and clean as other garments, so it doesn't matter quite so much if they have a small stain. This may be related to another feature that makes them low-maintenance, which is that most people don't iron jeans even when they do iron other types of trousers. As with all these statements, this is only a partial generalization. There are people who do iron jeans, especially mothers who iron jeans that their children would not bother ironing for themselves. But in general ironing is much less expected of jeans than of any other garment.

This idea that jeans may become dirtier and that this matters less links them to their practicality for work and is further bolstered by the idea that denim is a stronger or tougher textile. Of course, this particular attribute has been associated with jeans right from their invention as a new form of clothing. Recall that Levi Strauss took out a patent for the application of rivets to those areas of the trousers that were most likely to be ripped during heavy labor such as agricultural work and mining. Moreover, this attribute relates to the fabric itself, as the original denim used in these jeans was selected because it was particularly tough and coarse and therefore less likely to rip. The image of denim as a hardy fabric still persists today—for example, a participant talked about wearing jeans on a motorbike before they could afford to buy leathers, or "When I used to work on-site as an engineer before, I'd work in jeans, purely because the material is hard-wearing. If you catch it on something you wouldn't necessarily rip it, but with a normal pair of trousers you probably would." This is obviously also what makes them suitable for playing with children or gardening. For example, when someone says, "It's only recently when I've had children [that I wear jeans]. Obviously you can just throw them on. . . . They can get dirty, and the dirtier they are the better. And I find them comfortable with the children. It's only since I've had them that I've gone really into jeans." Here the word *comfortable* is used to express what is essentially a functional relationship.

The final consequence of this logic of the practical, which directly opposes jeans to issues of fashion or style, is the idea that jeans last longer than any other garment. Interestingly, this derives not from the idea that denim is harder than other materials but from the opposite idea, that it is softer, the point being that jeans actually become more comfortable over time as the cotton softens and starts to fit even better to the individual's shape and ways of moving in the world. Longevity is something most informants can attest to, referring to jeans they have had hanging in their wardrobes "forever," or discussing the ways in which they shop to replace worn-out clothes. Not only do jeans last longer despite being worn more often, but their place outside of fashion can also render them impervious to other factors that force people to shop more. For men in particular, who may regard all forms of shopping as something of a chore, this adds to the idea of jeans as comfortable, because it releases them from an uncomfortable task. Jeans thus are seen as comfortable in a more general sense of "not bothered" or "not having to bother." The fact that most of the jeans people possess are not expensive branded jeans but are high street shops' own brands or supermarket jeans combines with the idea that in lasting longer jeans save people money to render jeans practical, something that supports the household rather than becoming a burden or a chore.

This range of arguments with regard to jeans' practicality amounts to a legitimation for choosing jeans that is assumed to be largely pragmatic. As a result, people can come to believe that there is a natural logic to this preference, one that comes from intrinsic qualities of denim itself and its relationship to the qualities of its environment. This is then equated with the idea that they simply feel comfortable on the body. *Natural* here implies a largely instrumental or functional relationship to the world. The historical foundations for such a logic may lie in riveted trousers made of tough cotton fabric. Today, however, the logic is extended to jeans that (mainly in women's jeans) may have a significant addition of elastane fibers such as Lycra. This denim fabric often has a much lower weight and therefore is far less tough. But the idea that this denim stretches may be equally well suited to a concept of comfort linked to practicality. Moreover, almost all the jeans purchased by our participants have been subjected to a range of treatments that soften and weaken the fabric. So while the range of jeans includes those whose fabric remains tough, at least relative to other types of trousers, today denim is often not quite the fabric that it originally was. Despite these changes, this does not reduce the assumed and perceived relationship to practical comfort.

Examined a little more closely, many of the justifications people give for wearing jeans amount to tautologies. It is only the assertion that an attribute is natural that makes it so. Take, for example, the idea that jeans are practical because they need less washing or ironing or they can "hold the dirt." There is absolutely nothing intrinsic about denim that says it matters less for it to be ironed than, say, corduroy. There is nothing about the color indigo that makes it in some way naturally more suited to looking dirty than a pair of black chinos. There is no reason on earth why another population might not fetishize denim as something that must be kept pristine and neat, and see the dark gray wool we associate with suits as more natural in that it matters less if it becomes dirty. Nor it is obvious that dirt is less visible on indigo than on black or gray.

The same problem extends to the idea that people keep jeans longer because it matters less if they appear a bit torn and shabby compared to other garments. There is something unique about the way that denim ages, due to the dyeing process and how it is woven, that means that the white fibers become more visible and the fabric softens the more it is worn. The aging process results in a very changed garment from the original, one that is softer in feel and carries a different appearance. However, this could easily have had quite the opposite effect. Fading means that the age of jeans becomes more quickly apparent than with other trousers, and so they might be seen as lasting less long and needing replacement before other types of trousers where age takes longer to emerge on the garment itself. When other garments start to look shabby, they are thereby rendered unwearable and have to be thrown away. So there is actually an alternative logic that would suggest that, given their propensity to fade, jeans would be seen as lasting less long than other trousers. We have also seen that the fabric of many jeans today is lightweight and not particularly strong; for all those who argue jeans are good for one kind of climate, there are others who argue the opposite; and for every person who sees comfort as a precise fit to the body, there is another who sees comfort in the opposite idea, that jeans don't have to fit closely to the body. This diversity does not accord well with the notion of comfort that jeans brands employ. For example, brands such as Wrangler and Replay have a fit of jeans called "comfort fit." The idea of comfort here tends to imply a garment with greater ease (roominess) than the standard or "classic" offering. It is not surprising that this fails to accord with consumer definitions, since, as we shall see, for consumers comfort and fit have as much to do with social situations as with anything physical.

To recap, almost everything that has just been argued about the comfort of jeans, the practical and the pragmatic, comes not from any intrinsic quality of denim but from what we have designated as our attitude toward denim as a textile and indigo as a color. The decision whether one material or another is best when ironed is again arbitrary, just as it is when an elite considers that linen looks best when creased; it is not a quality of linen. A similar argument could be made about comfort being equated with as fitting well to the body. Jeans include some of the tightest trousers that anyone wears (skinny jeans) and also the least tight (baggy jeans). Similarly, new jeans made from heavy fabric that is 100 percent cotton are relatively rough and scratchy compared to polyester, for example, so we might have expected them to be regarded as particularly uncomfortable.

The word *comfort* appears to imply that a person has been released from all these issues of appearance, fashion, or cultural appropriateness, allowing us to return to arguments about practical things. Actually, this is almost entirely illusory. It works because historically there was once just such an association between jeans and practicality. But almost every single claim made for contemporary jeans as either practical or comfortable turns out on closer inspection to be all about appearance and cultural associations that have no such practical foundation. What we have actually documented here is the process of naturalization—how something cultural and arbitrary comes to be viewed and experienced as natural and incontestable. People really do believe that jeans don't need ironing, last longer, and can remain dirtier, all as a result of some physical property denim has. As we've noted, there is no reason why another society in another time might claim exactly the opposite to be the natural properties of denim. But once these processes of naturalization have taken place, then jeans do indeed have all the characteristics that people claim for them. And it is this that makes them so comfortable.

APPROPRIATE COMFORT

The complexity and ambiguity to be found in the idea that one wears jeans because they are the most comfortable of garments in terms of practical function becomes still more evident when one starts to examine a whole other array of uses of the word *comfortable,* those in which "being comfortable" refers to how a person feels in public or in the presence of others.

Many of our participants are quite explicit about the need to look acceptable under the gaze of others and how this is central to their ability to feel comfortable about themselves. Susan states: "You may have smart trousers but they're not as comfortable as denim. So you may feel like, 'I need to be comfortable for that day because I need to get to that state of mind,' and then you just put on the denims. So it's about a state of mind. I need to have the state of mind to wear that dress or else it's going to look wrong. I'll go out and be uncomfortable." People acknowledge a high degree of self-consciousness in public, under the gaze of the other, even when in some ways they would rather disown it. Says one: "I wear jeans to stay on a certain level so they wouldn't downgrade me for wearing another sort of clothes. Not that it matters much to me. It's just that I feel more comfortable that way." Another says, "You just have to wear something you feel comfortable with," and then immediately follows this with "People will look at you, and I say 'so what.' " As in several classic discussions of fashion (Simmel 1957; Wilson 1985), the paradox is that people recognize that this is simultaneously a process of conformity and one of individuality. But it is also an anxiety that is assumed to apply to pretty much everyone else: "You can't go into certain places with denim jeans. And equally— you see this on the street—a young person who's wearing denim in a certain way, I can imagine, would be uncomfortable walking about in certain parts of London. If they were walking, say, in Pimlico, Westminster, they would feel uncomfortable because of the way they chose to dress."

For younger people especially, the classic scenario, where one really doesn't want to feel uncomfortable, is at a party. And already it is possible to see ways in which being comfortable at a party links back to the idea that comfort is a practical issue, such as when someone says, "I've been to places where I wished I *was* wearing jeans. Like to a club or a bar. You feel more comfortable. You can dance around better. They're easier and so on," or another says, "But if I'm going to a house party then I would wear jeans . . . Because it's comfortable. At house parties you never know what's going to happen and you may have to leave. It's just to be comfortable and to be ready for anything." Sometimes the idea of wearing jeans to be appropriate is seen as a form of conformity, but others see it as a privileging of a more subjective feeling, one that is opposed to conformity: "In a party there is no particular rule as in what you should wear. If you wear what you feel comfortable, what you like, it's not what other people like, you don't have to follow them. If I want to wear jeans in the party, then I will wear jeans in a party. It's not like it is not allowed." The point is that once again the term used is *comfortable,* meaning that at least from the point of view of subjective experience there is a good fit with the situation. But that can mean a good fit because the person is wearing what others expect of him or her, or a good fit because the person is wearing what he or she wants to wear irrespective of what other people might think.

It could be argued that there are two entirely different semantic elements within the word *comfortable,* one pertaining to physical feelings or practical concerns and the other to a person's sense of his or her social surroundings. Comfort is far more multilayered in practice than is allowed through the concept deployed in advertising. But there are good reasons to reject this dualism and instead see it as significant that the word *comfortable,* which can mean physically at ease with something, also speaks to the sense of being socially at ease. We imagine that many people would recognize that feeling entirely inappropriate and uncomfortable in a social situation accrues a physical quality, at the extreme rather akin to feeling sick. This is probably made most explicit by young people who wear the totally wrong thing to a party and are very uncomfortable, to the point of feeling ill. So the importance of the term *comfortable* lies the way it creates this elision between what might otherwise be regarded as two separate domains.

This logic can also be applied to the material of chapter 3, on fashion. We might assume that fashion and comfort are opposed concerns, each taking its place at the expense of the other, and perhaps even irreconcilable. Yet the power of the term *comfortable* to elide what otherwise might seem like very different or contradictory imperatives may extend here also, as can be seen in the following two quotations:

> Whatever was comfortable. I'd go for comfort. I'm not into fashion. I've always been like that. I go for what I can afford and what looks good.

I think they're really comfortable. And easy. Yeah. And they're quite fashionable. And everybody wears them.

More or less in the same breath, participants are confirming both that comfort is opposed to fashion and that, at least in the case of jeans, comfort lies also in their compatibility with fashion. Turning this from a contradiction to an analytical finding requires only an acknowledgment that feeling at one with fashion is for many women integral to the physical sense of feeling comfortable, because wearing something that "looks good" is exactly what fashion promises to its followers. What ultimately makes jeans comfortable is the idea of a garment that can do both these things at once and thereby performs a practical resolution of what otherwise might be a contradiction. Similarly, jeans are a garment where feeling comfortable in the sense of appropriate in a party or other social situation also means feeling comfortable physically and having the sense of well-being that lets one get up and dance.

A parallel point is very well made in a recent paper by Sassatelli (2011) in exploring how young people in Milan come to see jeans as sexually alluring. The ideas in her paper can be easily translated into English colloquial discourse through a consideration of the two meanings of the word *fit*. One meaning of the word is something that conforms well to the particular shape of one's body, and this is how it was used in the previous chapter. But more recently *fit* has come equally to mean that something has enabled one's body to come across as sexy. Sassatelli's argument goes through three stages. It starts with the issue of fit in relation to fashion, which is clearly of concern to young people in Milan, a fashion capital. But in the case of jeans this is less a concern with the particular style or brand of jeans or what is fashionable for that year or season. Unlike most other garments, it has become for them more a question of wearing jeans in a fashionable way than of wearing fashionable jeans. In this case that means an emphasis on the particular capacity of jeans in relation to the body. Jeans are seen as an instrument that can of itself change the appearance of the body. In Italy (and also in Brazil; see Mizrahi 2011) jeans are expected to be able to give prominence to the wearer's behind, or lift it and give it better shape. In London this may be a broader sense that jeans may help make the wearer's legs slim and hide any cellulite. The second stage then is what Sassatelli calls "mirror work," an activity equally prominent in Woodward's ethnography (2007). "Mirror work" refers to the time spent in examining the precise effect of the clothing on the body and the way it will make the wearer look when he or she goes outside and is exposed to the gaze of others.

The most important effect of mirror work is its consequence for a person's self-confidence with respect to how others will see him or her. In turn, confidence about one's body (in Milan, particularly confidence about how one's behind looks) is the basis for the sense that one can look sexually alluring and can convey to others this sexual potency. As a reader will find confirmed endlessly in the pages of popular magazines such as *In Style* or *Cosmopolitan*, the degree to which one is self-confident about the sexual attractiveness of one's body is the degree to which one becomes actually sexually attractive to others. At this stage the idea of fit has moved from a relationship to oneself into being positively appraised by others as sexually attractive.

This argument is easily replicated in our own research. For example, a woman states, "So while some say you should stop wearing jeans when you get fat—before I had my eldest, when I was single and slim, not like now—I used to believe that time, even that it was keeping my shape, and still I believe. . . . Because when you wear the freestyle clothing you can tell what you're wearing and how much you put on. But when you are wearing trousers, denim jeans, you can't tell." So for this participant the idea that jeans hold in the body becomes more important as she becomes less confident about her body.

Although it confirms the general relationship between feeling comfortable and confident about one's body, the example just cited is unusual in that most of our participants don't actually feel comfortable wearing jeans when they have put on weight. Sometimes the waist of a pair of jeans may accentuate the fat above the waist (what many informants refer to as "love handles").

> I bought it for him, but he wasn't very happy. As I said, he has put on weight as well, and he has got a big belly and he [*laughs*] doesn't look right [*laughs*].

> Yeah, I have massive love handles here, and there's a certain pair of jeans that were quite tight and they really accentuated them. I looked at myself in the mirror and I thought, "Why did I bother to put these on?" I know I've got a big bum, like I said, but I think that really fat people, with big fat bellies . . . Sometimes jeans can make you look bigger than you really are. So if you are slightly overweight.

These speakers remain relatively sympathetic to the situation even though jeans are clearly seen as inappropriate given a certain body size or type. But people occasionally express something much closer to open disgust, such as "Really big women—I think they look horrible in jeans."

Wife: Some of them come in and they've got stomachs hanging out

Husband: That's one thing I don't like. And especially pregnant women. I've got to turn me head because it makes me feel ill. It does. It's just not right! They've got jeans on right down below their navel—it doesn't look very nice.

What this issue of fat makes clear is that while jeans are considered to "work" for the wearer if they are appropriate, this idea may imply a certain boundary policed by a clear sense of what is *not* appropriate. In this case the wearer no longer possesses a necessary quality: a body that suits jeans. Says one informant, "I didn't go socializing in jeans, if you see what I mean, because I would not feel comfortable, because by that time my figure had changed. Mentally I would not have felt comfortable wearing them."

If the issue of fat works to set the boundary of who shouldn't wear jeans, then we also have evidence from the other end of the spectrum, where people are striving for some sense of perfection. In this case the jeans involved are not "regular" jeans, as discussed in the last chapter, but rather skinny jeans, and the ideal body is the one that fits easily in them. This can be illustrated by what one participant referred to as "sore thumb syndrome," associated with wearing jeans that are as tight as possible, so tight that the only way the wearer can get them on is by lying down on the changing room floor and using the thumbs to squeeze the buttons into their holes. Such ultratight jeans are clear testimony to the desire to be in fashion. Furthermore, it seems absurd to associate something like sore thumb syndrome with the idea of comfort. Yet therein lies our paradox. For those who suffer with sore thumb syndrome, it is the second meaning of the word *comfort* that they are striving for. A woman goes through this extreme physical discomfort to achieve a state she will describe as feeling "comfortable" when she goes out with her friends that evening. This example demonstrates a point we made earlier in this chapter: that the word *comfortable* is used as a mechanism for the incorporation of everything that one might think it repudiates, even actions that otherwise would be regarded as the epitome of the uncomfortable. We can also now see that this is a two-way process.

It's not just about getting the jeans to fit with the body; it can be just as much about getting the body to fit the jeans. And it is the latter that is more rigidly policed.

THE COMFORT ZONE

As we have said, the idea of being comfortable is often paramount in terms of what people want from their clothing. Jeans have the capacity to make people feel more comfortable than other garments because they can elide the physical idea of comfort with the social concern about how the wearer looks in public. People may worry that an alternative garment would render them unfashionable, or that conformity to fashion makes them appear stupid or oppressed. Jeans offer an escape from both worries by appearing to replace the issue of fashion with a regime of the practical and the natural. Being able to provide an instrumental logic behind their choice makes people feel more comfortable.

Looking still more closely at the mechanisms behind becoming comfortable, we find it is not just that the word helps people live with contradictions. It does this in a particular way. This is easier to see when we go outside the realm of jeans for a moment and consider how the word *comfortable* is used for a wide spectrum of issues in life. Being comfortable is increasingly employed as an ideal in the wider realms of politics and ethics. It is used to imply a spectrum along which a person finds his or her preferred position or range. For example, a parent may be aware that some teenage children are allowed to drink as much alcohol as they like, while others are not allowed to touch a drop. The parent will talk of where along this spectrum he or she feels comfortable in terms of the behavior of his or her own children. As another example, knowing that a political party has to juggle levels of taxation against levels of public expenditure, people will talk of the balance between these about which they feel most comfortable. This idea of balance is what in the last chapter we called the Goldilocks phenomenon—the spot that's "just right."

In such situations most people espouse a relatively liberal attitude with respect to the behavior of others. This is equally true in the realm of jeans. An example would be the issue of where and when it is acceptable to wear jeans. Quite a number of our participants said they would not feel comfortable wearing jeans to a religious service. They said they preferred to wear traditional South Asian clothing such as *sari* or *shalwar kamiz* to a mosque or temple, or saw jeans as inappropriate to wear to church, especially in the case of a Jehovah's witness. But often these same people were quick to remark that this was a personal feeling and that they did not have a problem with other people wearing jeans to church, or, for example, wearing jeans to a mosque with a long *kurta* or *kamiz* above, so that the degree to which jeans tended to outline the body and become immodest was obscured by the upper garment. They seemed concerned to show that being comfortable derives in part from their tolerance and lack of prejudice with respect to what other people do.

This liberalism and tolerance are rarely extended to the self, however. People's "comfort zone" tends to be rather narrow. Being comfortable is not so much a positive appraisal of their own position as the sense that they would be very uncomfortable if they strayed any distance from the area within which they feel secure or confident. For example, a suspicion that other people are looking at them can lead to discomfort. As a normative trajectory, people are thought to start with a relatively small comfort zone, which stabilizes and grows as they move on. So, for example, teenagers are expected to be more anxious about their bodies and how they look than their parents are. The ideas is that becoming comfortable with oneself is a gradual process that often takes years if not decades, but which should produce an expanding comfort zone.

The evidence from our research is that jeans are often an integral part of this formation of the self. They work through a process of objectification (Miller 1987), which Woodward (2007) applied to understand getting dressed as an act of interrogating and constructing the self through the material form of clothing. People do not create this relatively stable self within its protective comfort zone mainly through introspection. It is much easier to accomplish this task through a relationship with something that at first appears external to themselves, an aspect of their material culture. Jeans perform this existential task of helping people locate themselves and establish what they come to feel is their real or authentic selves. As people decide if an outfit is suitable for them, they are striving to reconcile what George Herbert Mead (1913) referred to as the "I" and the "Me."

In line with everything that has been said in this chapter, we would expect this process to start with function and pragmatism. Let us consider something as straightforward as the balance between tightness and looseness.

> All jeans with me have started off quite uncomfortable, but as I've worn them I knew they would sort of mold into my leg style. So

these have actually become quite comfortable now. I'd consider wearing them casually.

They were constricting at the time, but as you wear them they sort of stretch out and become more comfortable.

They get better with time. They just feel more comfortable.

What is clear from these three quotations is that comfort, in terms of fit to the body, is not naturally an initial condition but rather something that happens over time. One aspect of becoming more comfortable arises from owning and wearing a pair of jeans for a long period, during which they become familiar and part of one's routine. On being asked how long she has owned her favorite pair of jeans, one participant replies: "Oh, too long. I think my daughters hid them. They say, 'You have new ones, you've got lots of new ones, why can't you wear them?' But I just feel comfortable in them. I've had them for a long time. There's nothing wrong with them. You wear them and then you like them and because you don't put them away in a drawer and they're there in the morning. And they're comfortable and you're familiar with them." This is another example of naturalization.

Part of the process involves the fact that jeans become softer and more comfortable to the individual the longer they are worn—the denim fabric softens where the body has rubbed it, and it loses its harshness. But another part of the process is that the mere longevity of possession, irrespective of any change in feel and texture, makes something appear more personal and more closely associated with that individual. This is the ease of not having to think about what to wear—there is comfort in routine. These two aspects of the naturalization process contribute considerably to the overall association of jeans with comfort. This also may help to explain the finding in the last chapter that once people have found the precise type of jeans they specifically associate with themselves, they are desperate to replicate them when they need to buy new jeans, and they can become frustrated when the shops no longer stock them. Says one participant, "It takes time for the new ones to win you over completely because you've got that one and you're more comfortable with it. . . . I've got one pair and it's like forever I'm going for that."

This process would normally be represented as a developing relationship between a person and an external object—the longer people have a pair of jeans, the better the jeans feel. But participants' accounts soon make it evident that the idea of comfort as a growing relationship to the jeans also involves how people feel about themselves. Going back to the quote from the woman whose children hid her old jeans, this is something the children failed to appreciate about their mother. For her, jeans act as an objectification that allows her to see herself as increasingly comfortable with life more generally.

We will finish this chapter with two extended examples. It is perhaps easiest to navigate through the complexities we have highlighted through an extreme case study and then look at the light it sheds on a more mundane and typical trajectory. Of all the participants in our study, Yusuf was the most devout Muslim. This was evident when we first met him, as he had a flowing beard and wore pure white attire. Much of our conversation was about devotional matters and the attraction of Islam, as presented by someone who feels he has finally found himself through his devotion to his religion. Interestingly, however, in earlier years Yusuf had been a single-minded devotee of blue jeans. Between the ages of sixteen and twenty, Yusuf had been an aficionado of Japanese selvage jeans, going online to locate jeans by core Japanese selvage brands such as 45rpm, Sugar Cane, and Edwin, brands well known to those who frequent specialized denim websites but probably entirely unknown otherwise.

This intense interest in Japanese selvage denim was followed by his turn to religion and a trajectory of increasing religiosity that led him to become the Yusuf we met, the Yusuf who has since thrown away all his jeans. We are not trying to directly equate denim and Islam as objects of devotion, but the habitus of each is the same—that is, the logic of devotion itself. In terms of the process of becoming ever more religious, Islam (like Judaism) is extremely different from Christianity. The process is usually based much less on issues of faith and spirituality and much more on the logic of religious law, interpretation, and practice. Individuals become drawn into, fascinated by, and increasingly devoted to the intricate logics that are central to such religions. Similarly, if a person regards denim as an object of concern and becomes more and more invested in getting the right jeans, then there is a logic that will lead to Japanese selvage as the most esoteric and valuable jeans on the market.

One of the remarkable things about this intense interest in Japanese selvage jeans is that virtually no one else who lived in Yusuf's milieu had the faintest idea of their value. He told us that he didn't think he had a single friend, relative, or acquaintance at that time who would have recognized what he was wearing, so the process was entirely personal. There was no sense in which he was trying to impress anybody but himself. It really was an act of personal devotion. It does then seem reasonable to suggest that this was a process through which he was finding a self he could respect and identify with. The jeans become a precursor to the vastly more developed relationship that comes with his current devotion to Islam. We think it is not mere coincidence that an individual who is so devoted to his religion was previously so devoted to his jeans. The nature of these devotions consists in large measure in allowing himself to become ever more invested in the underlying logic that they manifest.

Yusuf is an extreme example, but he helps illustrate the wider argument we are making about the potential of jeans to become an instrument by which people come to see and develop a relationship with themselves. But everything in this chapter has suggested that this is more commonly created in a less thoroughgoing and less isolated endeavor and has more to do with the relationship to outside forces such as fashion, the body, and the opinions of others. Much more typical would be the case of Arya. A young woman who, like Yusuf, is from a South Asian background, Arya is particularly concerned with her sense that she is unusually short and thin compared to the idealized body that she regards as conventional. Her discussions of jeans are all about the process by which she can gradually come to terms with her own body through finding the perfect jeans: "As I've grown older I've seen that due to my frame and my height some things suit me better. Flares don't suit me because I'm really small—five foot—so flares just make me look smaller, whereas I found that skinny jeans make you look taller than baggy jeans. . . . Because I've got really small ankles, my skinny jeans don't fit me all the way down and if they do they look silly. So it has to be . . . tight on the top leg and then inevitably it's going to be looser as it goes down because you're thinner." This is someone who wears jeans pretty much every day and has really worked on finding the right jeans, ones that she can feel comfortable with. But Arya's idea of comfort is not everyone's. Because she wants jeans that give shape to her behind and thighs, she is usually wearing something that is very tight in these areas, sometimes so tight that they are hard to sit down in unless they are made with stretch fibers. She has particular ideals in view, such as the actress Eva Longoria of *Desperate Housewives,* who is also small but glamorous. For Arya to feel comfortable about herself, about who she is and how she can be, she must find a way to feel confident in public. The search for jeans that will help her feel this way takes up a major part of her life at present and demands some sacrifice in terms of both financial cost and what others would regard as comfort.

The point is not to make a judgment here. In an era of environmentalist angst about overconsumption, the idea that an existential struggle to find oneself is enacted through getting an exact fit between body and jeans may easily be dismissed as materialism. Yet we should be prepared to accept some affinity between these two examples. Arya and Yusuf are both trying to perfect a relationship—initially with jeans, but as Yusuf's story shows, this can be the precursor to other relationships. It is harder to dismiss something as mere materialism when Yusuf's devotion to getting the perfect jeans was in effect a dry run for his current devotion to Islam.

CONCLUSION

Spending a chapter to this one word, *comfortable*, is justified because it is the word that our participants use more than any other to express what they say is the single most important reason they wear jeans. The discussion has embraced three semantic fields within the single term *comfort*: (1) a more physical and instrumental meaning; (2) the need to feel comfortable, in the sense of appropriate, under the gaze of others within a public situation; and (3) the longer-term process by which people find a sense of who they are, their personal comfort zone. This point extends the conclusion of the last chapter on the struggle to find the "right" jeans. We can now see that this search is part of a deeper project in life: the achievement of a state people wish to be in most of the time, a state of being in which they are as comfortable as possible with the world around them.

The bridge between this and what we regard as the most important finding of our research—the discovery of the ordinary—comes from the observation that in all three of these semantic fields, being comfortable is defined in opposition to feeling self-conscious. Once again we can see this as an elision between the physical and the nonphysical. For many people, a garment that is comfortable is one that they essentially do not feel at all. They are conscious neither of the clothes nor of their body. This is not like the softness of cashmere, which is pleasant to feel; it is an absence of having to be conscious of a presence. Discomfort is something that through the sensation of touch reminds people of the presence of their body. Comfort is about being able to take that body for granted.

This is the physical equivalent of the loss of self-consciousness, which relates to our second genre of comfort. What makes people desperately uncomfortable is the imagined critical gaze of others (Woodward 2005). To the degree to which jeans protect people from the imagination of that critique, they can begin to stop thinking about themselves and just get on with life. Being overly self-conscious, because it is related to a lack of self-confidence, is seen as directly contributing to people's failures in social relations. In the third semantic field comfort involves a more subtle excision of self-consciousness, because it consists of actually creating the self. It means arriving at a point at which one can take oneself for granted as a person, comfortable with one's own beliefs, manners, and politics. It is the elimination of self-consciousness in the form of anxiety about who one thinks one is. It is an escape from the existential accusation of living in bad faith (Sartre 1969), accomplished in part through developing a relationship to what at first seems an external domain but is actually a route to the stabilizing of a comfortable self. This elimination of self-consciousness will become central in our discussion of the ordinary in the following chapter. Obviously this is not some ultimate elimination of self-consciousness, as in certain types of religious quest; we are not talking nirvana here. It is simply the common aspiration to a state in which people can say they feel pretty comfortable—with their clothes, with their social situation, and with themselves. But given that we are only talking about a pair of trousers, that is quite a profound contribution.

CHAPTER 5

Ordinary

THE DEMARCATIONS OF JEANS

To say that the most extraordinary finding of this research is the discovery of ordinariness is clearly to suggest that being ordinary is not something one can take for granted. As later chapters of this book will argue, it is an achievement that in some ways has taken thousands of years, and comes into its present form only through new technologies that give us an imagination of a global ecumene that has no precedent. However, for the purposes of this chapter we will remain close to our ethnographic material of people's relationship to their jeans, and the larger historical and philosophical context and consequences will come later.

In this chapter we will examine claims about where it is not acceptable to wear jeans and what this implies. We will then explore the trajectory by which jeans move from being a marked garment to what we will call the post-semiotic phase, where jeans lose their capacity for any particular meaning or signification and thereby become far more important. This will include a discussion of how this works rather differently for men than for women. Next we will consider another factor that complements these: the rise of a sense of ubiquity manifested in jeans as default clothing, a kind of ersatz uniform. Finally, these come together in the ways in which jeans more positively assert an identity as ordinary, though for most people ordinary is constituted not by this assertion but more by the freedom from concern documented in the last chapter and the freedom from identity documented in this chapter.

The issue of jeans demarcating a terrain of acceptability and unacceptability was broached in previous chapters. What is remarkably consensual, especially given the diversity of origins for the people on these streets, is the agreement as to what exactly these areas turn out to be. A question we routinely asked was whether there were any circumstances in which it was not acceptable to wear jeans. These divide into two main categories: workplaces where there are explicit or implicit rules about not wearing jeans and social events at which it is considered inappropriate to wear jeans. With regard to work, many places require uniforms or have a dress code that precludes jeans; these include supermarkets and some other retail outlets. In certain other cases jeans have become specifically associated with a category of work, such as being a truck driver. Jeans can become almost a uniform within certain kinds of labor, usually various kinds of manual labor. Most people accept without question that there are many occupations in which people are expected to wear suits or the equivalent, and that this may be rule-based. More interesting are companies where employees are specifically instructed, "You can wear anything you like except for jeans." One example of this is a bank; another is any hospital work that involves seeing a patient; a third is the police force and again refers to circumstance where an employee might meet the public. All of this makes jeans a strikingly marked type of apparel. The general rule seems to be that if one is employed in the background, where one does not engage with the public, then the wearing of jeans often may be acceptable. To wear jeans when seeing a patient, customer, or member of the public might imply a lack of effort or inappropriate lack of concern. Under these circumstances jeans may be seen either as scruffy or as preventing people from taking the wearer seriously.

The area of work in which jeans come across as a particularly contested domain is teaching, with a wide variety of opinions expressed. A male teacher at primary school has ten pairs, since this dominates his work wear. One teacher refers back to the 1950s as the period when his own opinions were formed. "In those days when I became a teacher I would always go dressed up. Other teachers . . . a teacher I remember used to wear denims with a hole in the backside with a shirt sticking out. I used to think that was just not acceptable. To me, going into a classroom like that was just not acceptable, but on the whole I was very conservative. I never actually changed a lot." Teachers in a contemporary private school suggest one can get away with occasionally wearing denim, but it would be frowned upon to wear jeans often. This is true even in contexts where people are told they can wear casual clothing, so somehow jeans are more casual than other types of casual attire. This seem to reinforce the idea that not wearing jeans is a mark of respect, mainly respect for others, but in teaching there also seems to be an implication of self-respect.

A frequently noted corollary of this common ban on wearing jeans at work is that jeans often thereby became the natural thing to change into after work. For example, a cab driver who feels it is inappropriate to wear jeans during work hours changes into them as soon as he comes home. Obviously there is a kind of chicken-and-egg argument here: jeans are not permitted at work because they have become associated with leisure, and they become even more associated with leisure because they are forbidden at work. For others, arriving home from work means changing into tracksuit bottoms, whereas jeans are for casual social occasions.

Within the nonwork arena, almost everyone mentions weddings as times when jeans could be inappropriate. One woman told the story of her wedding, which was not in a church, and a friend of her husband's niece "wore jeans. I would never notice until it was pointed out by my husband. He made a comment on it. And I thought: 'Why, he looks smart, what's the problem?' It never went into my head, but Peter had noted it as inappropriate." This woman was quite exceptional in that she was one of the few people who claimed she would wear jeans to a wedding, but in her case she added she would not wear them to church. After weddings, the next most common example of a jeans embargo was funerals. Others suggested a baptism or a job interview. Households that included people from South Asia and West Africa noted a preference for wearing traditional dress for more formal family occasions.

More contested was the issue of wearing jeans at church. One factor here was age—people assume that the younger someone is, the more acceptable it is to wear jeans even at quite formal occasions. Another factor people note is that if someone does wear jeans, they can be dressed up to look more formal, such as wearing them with a jacket or, for a woman, a long top. A family from Sierra Leone recalls a wedding when someone not only wore jeans to a wedding but wore ones with "rips on this side and also on the behind and on the bottom," which was deemed to not be "proper." The woman in question "ended up leaving the wedding anyway . . . because some were quite brazen and they told her. She had to leave." It was therefore not just the wearing of jeans, but the style of them, and also that they were worn with a "skimpy top." As our informant says, "If the jeans were not so much designer but presentable, it would have been appropriate," and that "if it had been late at night it would have been okay. But it was during the day. It was a very expensive hotel."

With regard to church, it also depends on denomination, with groups such as the Salvation Army, Jehovah's Witnesses, Baptists, and Pentecostals being more conservative in this regard. People recall a time when there were restaurants where jeans were not acceptable and occasions such as going to the theater when it was frowned upon to wear them, but this is increasingly seen as anachronistic, with people commenting that one would have to find an unusually formal restaurant today for this to present a problem. It still can happen: "We were looking for somewhere to eat and we got into one of these hotel foyer restaurants. And it was very formal, and they stressed that I was wearing jeans. And finally they let me in, but I didn't really enjoy it, because of that." Some still don't wear jeans to the theater; one person would wear jeans to stand at the Globe Theatre, but not to sit in a West End theater.

In general, the reason jeans should be avoided at formal occasions is much the same as the one that pertains to work. One participant notes, "A friend of mine died in a diving accident two months ago, and somebody turned up in the pub afterwards in a pair of jeans and there was a lot of comments—they're all around my age—about how he was in jeans even though he had a shirt on." The problem was that jeans were deemed to indicate a lack of respect. Blue jeans in particular are inappropriate; a pair of black jeans in such a situation would appear to be a little more acceptable.

Rather different from this are the more personal rules that people create for themselves that help them construct marked occasions through the medium of not wearing jeans. This may refer simply to the idea of dressing up as for a party or otherwise going out in the evening. If the whole point is to make the occasion feel special, then wearing jeans is seen as a failure to make the requisite effort. As one person put it, "There's so few things you can actually dress up [for], why wear a pair of denims?" For others, jeans were associated with being "casual, going out to the shops," or maybe a trip to the cinema, but not "going *out* out," or as someone else put it, not "when I went really out." In most cases, these are people who wear jeans as their main casual clothing and need to differentiate within their clothing in order to construct a marked occasion, such as the previous examples of dressing up for the theater. As has been discussed previously, jeans derive their meaning for people through combination and contrast with other items in the wardrobe. For some young people, the issue is not their sense of occasion but one of dressing appropriately according to the conventions of the occasion and what everyone else is wearing. This includes the expectation that women will wear a dress or skirt to go out in. There is the potential for embarrassment by not dressing up, as one woman puts it: "Well [*laughs*], we went to a concert at Hammersmith Odeon and I had on jeans, but when we got there the first crowd of people we seen was young black girls and they were dressed to the nines [*laughs*], and I thought, 'Aw, gosh! I've put these jeans on!'"

As we will see, there are also those who wear clothes other than jeans at home to signify relaxed wear, which make jeans available as a mark of dressing up. But for those who wear jeans to go out in, there is a common differentiation within their jeans, as in "You'd have two types of jeans. One to go out in and one to lounge around in." Another young woman tries not to wear her "good jeans" around the house so as not to spoil them. Once these best jeans have been worn for a while, they may be relegated to everyday wear and replaced with something new. The other option is to transform jeans into being dressy through accessorizing.

The issue with getting dressed up, then, is not generally one of respect, but more of marking certain occasions or times of day as special. An area that bridges these two genres of jeans avoidance is dating. Paramount for women would be how to make the best of their body (discussed in previous chapters), so if jeans make their behind look good, they would wear them, but if it looks too big in jeans, they would avoid them. There was, however, also a sense that if one wanted to show a potential partner that one was making an effort, then jeans were not appropriate and again didn't really show respect. As one young man put it, "If it is the first meeting, you get to know someone, they are supposed to appreciate that you can relax with them. And jeans are supposed to be for relaxing. If it was to me personally, I wouldn't care. But in terms of convention, I think the first time you're supposed to wear something special. But if you're going out with someone you know, say, the person you married, then denim is probably the best thing." Indeed, when he talks about attraction to girls when he is out, he says, "I certainly wouldn't pick someone who was wearing jeans." He goes on to suggest that a girl who is dressing to go out with a boy should accentuate her femininity by wearing feminine clothes, and wearing jeans misses, in a way, the point of a potential date.

The overall conclusion from this evidence is summarized by a participant who said that it would be okay to wear jeans "if there was no meaning to where I was going, if where I was going there was no point in dressing." To wear something other than jeans is often an act of signification, whether of respect, identity, or occasion. But if the category of "other than jeans" signifies something, then there is some sense in which wearing jeans is an act without signification,—a strange claim that at this point still sounds implausible. The task of the next section is to provide convincing evidence that this could be the case.

THE POST-SEMIOTIC GARMENT

Semiotics is the study of signs and signification, the idea that something stands for or represents something else. Semiotic approaches, especially those deriving from Saussure and characterized by Barthes in *The Fashion System* (1967), have been applied extensively to clothing (such as in Sahlins 1976), as particular items of clothing are taken as standing for attributes, such as sexiness, danger, or (in the case of jeans) America. Notwithstanding critiques of such approaches, both in terms of the particular form of semiotics it assumes (Keane 2005) and in terms of semiotics failing to pay heed to the materiality of clothing (Woodward 2005), there is some use in the approach when considering the historical associations of jeans. The idea of jeans as a post-semiotic garment implies a long trajectory, starting in a time when they certainly were a semiotic garment, drenched in symbolism and meaning. We collected some wonderful stories from some of our older informants. In chapter 1, we introduced an elderly man who thought he was among the first in the area to obtain a pair of blue jeans, from a U.S. soldier during the war, and a woman who was beaten up by other women around 1958–59 because she had the effrontery to wear a pair of jeans.

Clearly, the first core semiotic marker for jeans was their association with America. Jeans first entered the United Kingdom as a clear sign of Americanization. First they were generically American; then they became associated with transgressive or rebellious youth, initially through American icons such as James Dean and Marlon Brando. But then came the first wave of British jeans made by companies such as Lee Cooper in the 1960s, which corresponded to the British version of youth counterculture associated with Carnaby Street. This association with transgressive youth lasted for quite some time but has now disappeared. The authority to pronounce on this came from one of our participants, who works for the police. He was quite clear as to whom he would keep an eye out for today: kids in hoodies, tracksuit bottoms, and so forth. He recalls there was a time when wearing jeans, certainly those in the hip-hop style or highly distressed ones, might have meant this was someone to look out for, but no longer. Similarly, jeans' association with the United States is now viewed as entirely historical. No one wears jeans today in order to appear more American or in reference to the United States.

So jeans started off as marked, and today it is possible for them to remain marked in various ways. The most obvious of these is the semiotic signification of particular kinds of jeans. One form of marked jeans is designer jeans. If the brand is visible, then the jeans can be recognized and interpreted as special or marked. If it is not visible, simply knowing that one is wearing that brand may make the wearer feel special. The same is true of particular styles, especially when the style is more extreme, such as extremely skinny jeans or the extremely baggy jeans associated with hip-hop. This often has the desired effect on others, such as an older man who comments, "I hate the look, you know, when they wear them and they're halfway down there."

As noted in chapter 3, many people, especially women, possess such marked jeans: branded jeans, skinny jeans, jeans that are for going out or for special occasions. But these are not the jeans that most people wear most of the time. So it seems reasonable to give more attention to the jeans they don't talk about very much, the ones that don't express some particular style or brand but are in fact what they wear most of the time. Turning to these jeans, we can clearly discern another underlying trend: that bit by bit, the jeans that most people wear most of the time are losing their semiotic markers and thereby turning into something no other garment has ever achieved, a genuinely post-semiotic status—an absence of symbolic status, which, as we have seen, makes them inappropriate for occasions classified as marked.

To achieve this state, jeans needed to lose their historical association with the United States, transgressive behavior, and any particular group of people. One hugely important achievement with regard to British society was when jeans progressed from being claimed to be classless to actually being classless. Indeed, if one was to predict who might be wearing an expensive brand of jeans today, it is more likely to be the maid than the mistress. In Miller's other studies (e.g., 1998, 2008), few people within the middle classes are found to wear branded jeans, which are regarded as vulgar. But he has come across such jeans when working with the Filipina cleaners (Madianou and Miller, in press) who work in such households, something that probably reinforces the disdain for designer or branded jeans within the dominant social fraction.

More important is the evidence (discussed in previous chapters) that the vast majority of jeans people today buy are not branded in any significant way. What people seek out and wear are what they call "classic," "regular," or "standard" jeans—what was also referred to in chapter 3 as "proper jeans," "real jeans," or, even more significant, "just jeans." What was clear from our research is that when one sees a person wearing that kind of jeans, one learns nothing at all about that person. Such jeans are no longer evidence of any kind of position with respect to British society more generally. As discussed in chapter 4, these jeans are comfortable partly because they don't stand out in any respect. A corollary to this is that jeans are seen as compatible with even those groups who try to manifest difference in the extreme. As one person put it, "The chavs can wear jeans. Goths wear black jeans. Every sort of type of person, not just age, can all wear jeans in their own style. Grunge is really baggy jeans. Everybody can dress them in a different way." The implication is that jeans are a kind of canvas that can be painted on to produce creative styles, but this works only to the extent that jeans in themselves appear as the blank canvas beneath such work. This role in transcending difference then becomes even stronger testimony to their inclusive nature.

There is now no age group that does not wear jeans. We find clear instances of association with jeans at both the earliest and oldest of ages, as in the following two examples. A woman talked about her husband, who constantly equates being in fashion with wearing jeans. At one point she exclaimed, "As soon as my son was born he [her husband] went and bought him some jeans that were this size. They were so uncomfortable for a baby, but he wanted to see his son in jeans right away. So he [the baby] had this big nappy and this little bottom and he looked really strange." At the other end of the spectrum a woman talks of her sixty-one-year-old partner who always wears jeans since he is trim. Even at that age, he doesn't so much wear jeans as use them to flaunt his body. She said, "If you ever wanted to make an advert about older people in jeans, he'd be the person to make the advert with. And he never wears anything else."

In both cases it seems important for these men to make the assertion that jeans are no longer associated with a particular age group—everyone has a kind of natural entitlement to wear jeans from the cradle to the grave. It is also significant that the older people we interviewed generally did not wear jeans when younger but only started wearing them frequently within the last decade or two. Jeans may well signify a genuine shift that makes elderly people more effectively integrated into the mainstream than previously. This image may be helped by aging rock stars who can still be almost cool or by the insistent energy of the baby boomers, but in any case it has become harder and harder to exclude older people. However, it is worth noting that despite such changes, fashion still aims to attract the young, most clearly exemplified in how jeans are marketed and advertised.

Perhaps the final frontier in terms of exclusivity is the prejudice against overweight people wearing jeans. This probably remains more common than not. In chapter 1 we provided several stories of people who felt they couldn't wear jeans when they put on weight, or who saw jeans as their reward for losing weight. But even this final prejudice seems to be in decline. Anyone who has traveled to the United States knows that it is possible for jeans to become the regular attire of even those who in the United Kingdom and continental Europe would be regarded as clearly overweight. But when this prejudice against girth dies away, there will be no variant of humanity who is seen as in any way an unnatural bearer of blue jeans. At that point it seems reasonable to talk of jeans becoming post-semiotic inasmuch as they no longer signify any particular social fraction or group.*

ORDINARY MEN AND ORDINARY WOMEN

The process of jeans becoming post-semiotic is not yet complete, and there is at least one very manifest distinction that remains: there is a striking contrast between being an ordinary woman and being an ordinary man. For women to use jeans to opt out of all relationships to both fashion and the need to dress for the occasion would be anything

---

* We would willingly concede that within the discipline of semiotic studies this concept of the post-semiotic would not be acceptable. People with expertise in this area, such as Webb Keane, have reminded us that there can be no such thing as the truly post-semiotic, and (as will become clear in our discussion) jeans do in fact signify a state of ordinariness, which is itself a form of semiosis. But we would argue that, even if technically incorrect, the use of the term *post-semiotic* is justified in this case because it clarifies the way in which jeans become ordinary by having escaped from all other forms of signification.

but ordinary. As we found in chapter 3, the ideal quality of jeans for many women lies in their ability to resolve the contradictions of fashion: the contradiction between conformity and individuality, and that between sameness and difference more generally. The single most common way for this to be achieved is through seeing jeans as a kind of uniform or foundation over which the rest of the clothing is applied as differentiation. So wearing jeans doesn't diminish a woman's concern and anxiety with the rest of what she wears when she is going out clubbing or even just getting dressed for work. Because jeans have lost their own specificity, they can just as easily become casual or dressy depending upon how they are accessorized with other clothing such as a top or with a belt or shoes. A similar effect can be achieved by wearing a particular style of jeans, such as skinny jeans.

From when she was very young, jeans were a constant in Florence's life. This was the item of clothing she could always relate to, while it also retained enough of a fashion dynamic to keep her interested. She talks of the all-in-one denim bodysuits with images of the women from *Charlie's Angels* on them that she loved when she was eight, and jeans with big flares. As she grew older she became aware that her mother also wore jeans all the time, and she needed to differentiate herself. That was not a problem: since her mother always wore cheap standard jeans, she started to buy branded fashion jeans such as Levi's. Today she has five pairs of jeans in addition to cropped jeans and denim skirts. She feels she can now combine these with a wide range of accessories to meet more or less any occasion, She constantly refers to dressing up or dressing down jeans. An example of the former would be combining jeans with a black sparkly top and a pair of high boots. Only blue jeans have this quality; jeans in other colors, such as black, do not. She is quite clear that not only does this mean she can always remain sufficiently in fashion for her purposes while retaining the constancy of jeans but also that this satisfies her personal contradiction between individualism and conformity and between blending in with a crowd and standing out from that crowd.

The conversation takes a marked turn, however, when it comes to describing her husband. Jeans are even more ubiquitous in his life than they are in hers, in that he never wears anything but jeans if he can help it. But, in stark contrast to her, he does not make any attempt to relate his jeans to fashion or distinctions of any kind. As she says, "I've tried to get him a bit more fashionable, but he won't have it. He says, 'I'm not sixteen. They're for sixteen-year-olds, not for me.'" All he will ever wear is what she regards as boring: classic middle-aged men's jeans, pale blue basic Levi's, the kind that in an earlier chapter was associated with the "Jeremy Clarkson effect." This pretty much extends to her children also. She feels she has far more flexibility when it comes to giving her daughter a diversity of clothing, but with her son she finds it hard to think what he could ever wear apart from denim. So she retains some sympathy for her husband, but still regards his obsession with jeans as more to do with his refusal of difference than with any genuine constraint resulting from lack of choice in the shops.

This reinforces a point made in chapter 2. A woman cannot strive to be unmarked by always wearing the same type of jeans in the way most men can. She is likely to experience several different contexts that all demand a different type of jeans. So she needs to find the jeans that are ordinary to these specific contexts if she wishes to remain ordinary overall. With men it is usually different. Oroon can't wear jeans at work, nor does he wear them to the Hindu temple, but his wife notes he has a whole wardrobe of essentially similar jeans because it's all he ever wears at any other times. Richard sees jeans as such a staple that clothes shopping simply consists of buying several pairs of jeans at one time. Another phenomenon associated only with men but found in several cases was the kind of superubiquity of Levi's. We even found individual men nicknamed "Levi's" or just "Jeans" since that is all they ever wear. Levi's possess a potential for this kind of core ubiquity partly through their bedrock 501 style. With some men, one almost feels they were born and will die in Levi's 501s, making the expression "I wouldn't be seen dead in anything else" perhaps literally true. (Though we did have one participant who was firmly within this niche, but then "had a fling" with a pair of Wrangler jeans, fell for them, and from then on has only ever worn Wrangler.)

Some women, of course, do come closer to the male sense of simple ubiquity. A woman talks of a period when jeans took over her life completely, since they seemed perfect for the kind of work she was doing, which could include crawling on the floor to empty cash machines. This subsequently extends to a notion of casual that brooks no deviation. She would never buy dressy jeans or choose a top and accessories to make her jeans dressy; she just wore plain jeans, boots, and a clean top and that was that for all occasions, which pretty much corresponds to the male sense of ordinariness.

By the same token, there were men who were ordinary in the sense we have just generalized as female. A woman described her husband as being obsessed with jeans—he wore nothing else and had a vast array of them, twenty or thirty pairs. She described these jeans as all blue but also all different: "Sometimes they have brown weird designs on them, or different kinds of rips. There's something different about every kind of pair." As with women generally, it's not just the diversity, but the concern to dress them up or down according to the occasion. "If going to a club, he'll wear it with a shirt and a blazer with shoes. If casual, he might wear them with trainers."

DEFAULT AND UBIQUITY

Everything that has been said so far in this chapter—indeed, all the generalizations made in the previous chapters—can of course be refuted. They are partial generalizations with scope for considerable variation and rejection. If this were a study in the natural sciences, any generalization we made would be wrong, since there are always going to be examples that contradict these generalizations. If half the population of the United Kingdom is wearing jeans on any given day, of course there will be vast numbers of exceptional cases. Yet as we are social scientists, not natural scientists, we take responsibility for picking out the main flow and asserting its significance despite such exceptions. In this case, we are prepared to assert that on the basis of our evidence, jeans are approaching a post-semiotic status. This does not imply that such a state will ever be fully achieved in the sense that everyone will suddenly conform to such a massive generalization. Clearly some people buy designer jeans. We choose to be more interested in the evidence that hardly anyone in the streets where we did our fieldwork actually wears them, even when they possess them.

The post-semiotic condition is only one side of our argument for ordinariness. The other comes more directly from Woodward's earlier ethnography of how women choose clothes to wear more generally (2007) and was one of the catalysts for choosing this new research topic. This was her discovery that denim could be considered a kind of default mode for simply getting dressed and out of the house in the morning. The word *default* seems appropriate to the phenomenon, central to Woodward's first study, in which women getting up in the morning first decide to wear some other form of clothing, usually something more individual in appearance, but then, having looked at themselves in the mirror and lacking confidence about how they will appear in those clothes, take them off again and put on jeans. Many of our participants testified to this as well. "Sometimes I prepare my clothes the night before. This one time I thought I'd wear a top with a skirt. The skirt was up to here. The next day when I saw it I thought it was not right. I want the top but I'm not comfortable with the skirt today. So I just get one of the baggy jeans and wear that. So that's fine. Because I was going to work and I needed to be comfortable." The role that jeans play in the wardrobe relates in part to the frequency of wear, and jeans are repositioned and given a different meaning after they have been worn over a long period of time. The default mode can be legitimated as showing that a woman doesn't care much about clothes and how she looks. Yet when Stevie is discussing his girlfriend, he notes that she often ends up in jeans precisely because she is so concerned to feel that she looks good when she goes out.

The concept of default in the sense of reliance upon jeans may well connect with the desire to retain them, as when Charlotte says, "Yeah, [they're] like a kind of safety blanket. You can't throw them out really because you wear them most of the time." This links with the idea that they are timeless and always going to remain in fashion, as well as with the idea that they are easier to shop for since it doesn't matter so much if they don't fit perfectly. In other words, the use of jeans as a default merges with the idea that they are both ubiquitous and nondescript, all of which can be seen as meaning that jeans have achieved an unmarked relationship to time as well as to everything else. This is the way jeans achieve a paradoxical status as the garment that is in fashion because it is always in fashion, essentially nullifying the dependence of fashion upon change or a specific relationship to the moment. Jeans are timeless as well as ageless.

The distinction drawn above between males and females can also extend to and even reinforce this default mode. A woman noted of her husband: "I say, 'I don't know what to wear.' And he says, 'Oh, wear your jeans.' Really, they're like good old faithfuls, aren't they?" One can imagine many men feeling positively disposed toward jeans precisely because jeans help them avoid being drawn into women's anxieties over what to wear. This may be stereotypic of gender relations, but our evidence suggests that at least in this case it remains typical. And this is not necessarily an opposed position, since women remain generally responsible for the laundry and cleaning for the entire household. As a result, the fact that the grandparents are now wearing jeans, the kids will be satisfied as long as they have a clean pair of jeans, and the husband never changes into anything else means that the whole chore of household laundry is greatly simplified to a cycle of throwing jeans into the washing machine and not even having to iron them. So although at one level these women might like their husband and children to be less boringly ordinary, from a domestic labor point of view there are clear compensations,

A further example of this came with the issue of school uniforms. In previous research Miller has carried out on London streets (1998), he was surprised to find out how much most parents preferred the idea of their children's school having a uniform, while teachers tended to oppose the idea, largely on liberal grounds. For the parents the issue was one of convenience and the avoidance of incipient status rivalries that can develop when fashion becomes an issue. With a school uniform they were freed from the anxieties of their children choosing what to wear for school. Uniforms were also seen as simplifying the laundry and being relatively easy to repair when, inevitably, clothes got torn at school or the knees wore through. Several remarked that at that time they had more or less promoted the idea of the children wearing jeans as a kind of pseudo uniform for precisely these reasons. In one case the children subsequently rebelled and refused to wear jeans at all. In other examples children had a school uniform but changed into jeans the moment they returned home, so that jeans managed to be both a rejection of uniform and a continuation of it at the same time. One child reported that at school he was told that they ought to wear jeans because the school didn't have a uniform in the sixth form. It was not just the parents who preferred the idea of a school uniform: in many cases the children too recognized that they could become quite anxious without a uniform because of the competition and opportunities for disparagement that could otherwise emerge. Though an actual school uniform seemed to be something they should have grown out of, when they were in the sixth form jeans once again provided the solution: the uniform that isn't formally a uniform.

It is not much of a stretch to go from this idea of a uniform to the general idea of jeans as ubiquitous. As one of our participants says, "You don't have to worry about things when you wear them. You can't tell a person's class or income. . . . It's a modern-day uniform." For adults, part of the motivation can also be this same anxiety about wearing anything but jeans. Another person says, "I find that people notice you for what you wear rather than who you are as a first impression. The informant continues, "Everybody looks good in jeans, below a certain age, under fifty. And nobody is going to criticize you because of your choice." He sees jeans as a "safe option." He sees jeans as being something some girls may find attractive, but on the whole "I think they look at [the jeans] and it's not attractive but it's not repelling. So they look at you and they go, 'Hmmm, it's worth an approach.'"

It is as though the sense of ubiquity is established around jeans as a pseudo-uniform at school. That sense is just as strong, if not stronger, during the college years. And, as we shall see in more detail below, it can also be central to the idea of then becoming an ordinary housewife or worker, or trying to achieve a general state of relaxation. Finally, jeans become something one can wear when one is retired, and they are perfect for gardening. In other words, every phase of life has its specific condition that makes jeans not just ubiquitous but particularly appropriate to the needs of that stage. Seen from a wider perspective, jeans manage not to signify age or stage.

If we put together these various observations—jeans as post-semiotic, jeans as uniform, jeans as default, and jeans as ubiquitous—we are in a position to confirm something that was implied at the very end of the last chapter: that jeans can accomplish an existential task, an experience tantamount to a loss of self-consciousness. This was expressed in a wide variety of ways, such as "It's the type of thing that you get up in the morning, you put on your clothes, and they are jeans. You know? They are not thought as to. They are just something you put on." There are various versions of this sentiment, ranging from "not having to think about it" to the quality of thoughtlessness ascribed to doing up one's shoelaces—that is, it just happens. "If you're not going anywhere particularly interesting, they're easy because they're quick. You know what you can wear with it. I probably do end up wearing the same pair more often than others." One person noted that jeans represented "switching off": switching off from school, switching off from work, and so on. "They're great for changing into after school, because they represent the separation between serious school and coming back and relaxing." While for women this lack of thought was most often discussed in terms of getting dressed, men saw this more in terms of going shopping. "I'd just go to a Levi's shop because I couldn't be bothered to think. . . . I wasn't really too into looking at . . . clothes in the old days." This ideal of the thoughtless automaton often seems to equate loss of consciousness with an implied triumph over the burden of self-consciousness.

ORDINARY CLOTHES AND ORDINARY PEOPLE

The final stage in this argument is the demonstration that this quality of the ordinary then becomes naturalized as though it were an intrinsic quality of the garment itself and/or of the people themselves. For most people, the ubiquity of jeans seems to emanate naturally from what they assume to be the fundamental nature of jeans, an integral quality of the garment. Again and again people inform us that one of the main reasons they wear jeans is simply that jeans can go with anything at all—any color, any type of garment. In response to this, we ask people to imagine that they are wearing another pair of trousers of a different material but exactly the same indigo color as jeans, and then we ask if these too would go with any other garment or any other color. People tend to have a little think about this but then always affirm that such trousers wouldn't go with anywhere near as many colors or types of garments as jeans do. We then ask them to imagine that they are wearing a pair of denim jeans but of some color other than blue. Would these denim jeans go with any other color or fabric? Again they usually reply in the negative. What these two questions demonstrate is that the assertion that denim blue jeans are compatible with all other garments cannot arise either from some property of denim or from some property of indigo. The reason that jeans can indeed be matched with practically anything is that they have achieved this quality of post-semiotic insignificance: there is nothing for other garments to clash with or match with. When blue jeans become nothing in themselves they can go with anything. And the fact that they can go with anything is the final evidence that they have become post-semiotic. But this is not something any wearer of jeans is aware of. They always insist that being able to go with anything must be some property of the blue jeans themselves, and are quite shocked if we then reveal that this cannot be the case.

When we turn from an attribution of ubiquity to the garment and instead consider the attribution of ubiquity to people, jeans take on a further quality of radical egalitarianism. "Jeans are for everybody. I think it's lovely. Even for small babies, for kids. Even for older people." This is an ordinariness that many people wish to identify with, but commensurate with the term *ordinary,* this identification is rarely an assertive or activist form of association. Radical egalitarianism is not a concept that would instantly occur to these participants. Rather, we hear a quiet and modest claim to occupy some kind of untroubled middle ground of existence that is entirely unobtrusive. One way in which this is signified is through buying jeans at Marks & Spencer, which at least for men has garnered a reputation for being outside fashion or significance, much to the chagrin of its marketing department. Two of our informants remarked on this. One said, "Lawyers in my experience are quite conformist. The uniform there really was a kind of jeans and jumper from Marks & Spencer, or something like that. Jeans was the main thing." And a woman in her fifties working as a mealtime supervisor at a school found Marks & Spencer her solution, having gone through twelve different pairs trying to find jeans that were sufficiently ordinary. What she wanted was the epitome of comfort, as described in the last two chapters—jeans that were not marked by any feature at all. It went with her unassuming home furnishings and plain, unpretentious manner.

When someone says, "It's just easy. They go with everything," and it is clear that they therefore wear jeans pretty constantly. there is an elision between the idea that the jeans go with anything and the idea that the person goes with anyone. Jeans convey the ideal of being a simple, unaffected, everyday kind of person, friendly and inoffensive, someone who could be included in what we called in the introduction the "silent community." Jeans cause no bother physically or socially. This is often the position of the middle group, those who are neither young nor old, who are just workers and housewives. Vicky is quite clear about this: "When I started wearing denim it was because I wanted to stand out less. . . . I really wanted not to be looked at so much, I went in for being much more conformist after that." Two things prompted this decision. One was a reversal of a previous teenage period when she had tried being a Goth, and the other was a year living in China when she felt she had been stared at all the time. "I wanted to be less conspicuous and fitting more with everyone else was wearing, and that was mostly jeans." As another woman put it: "I do like Marks & Spencer. Their branding is quite good, the stitching. Good value. I think it's our upbringing. We were always single-parent, low-income. We always look out for sales, have a budget. We never splashed out, really, and we're still the same. If it's on sale, we'll buy it."

Clearly Marks & Spencer marks a kind of hyperordinariness, just as Levi's well-known 501 style marks a male hyperubiquity. Most people need not resort to either. Actually, when it comes to blue jeans we found that most people barely know what they are wearing—the brand, the place where they bought them, or anything else. One of the most remarkable findings was how little most people seemed to know about the item that they wore most often, not only not remembering what brand they were, but even whether or not they were a brand. Clearly that is also why people wear them. They are just jeans, just ordinary, because the people wearing them are ordinary people, nothing special, not even especially or hyper ordinary.

The appropriate question a skeptic should always pose to academic work is, so what? Should it surprise us that being ordinary is an aspiration? Does it matter very much, anyway? So far we have concentrated upon the way people and jeans achieve ordinariness in the contemporary world. The rest of the book will show why this matters. While later we will turn to more esoteric academic and philosophical arguments for why the ordinary matters, in the next chapter we will remain within the ethnographic framework, because first we need to establish that ordinariness matters a great deal for the people we have been discussing so far. We need to show how and why people struggle toward this status and how important, often how positive, this can be in terms of their wider life. There are reasons why jeans have been co-opted as a weapon toward this end, but we need to understand the battle they are helping us to win.

CHAPTER 6

The Struggle for Ordinary

INTRODUCTION

The evidence in this book suggests that being ordinary is far from something to disparage. It is not a failure to be special. It is actually a state most people in this study aspire to, at least for some of their lives, a state that may or may not be difficult to achieve. The last chapter ended with examples of people for whom being ordinary doesn't seem to pose much of a problem. It is something of a given in terms of how they are situated themselves and how they are situated by others; they occupy a kind of median position within a range of difference. People's aspiration in this direction was conveyed through their identification with jeans from shops such as Marks & Spencer, which appears to represent what a variety of individuals, whose work ranges from that of a lawyer to a school meals attendant, might see as the epitome of the unspecial. Marks & Spencer seems to occupy a niche that once was seen as middle-class but perhaps is now better understood as middle-culture and is very likely also associated with that other aspiration of the median, suburbia. A working class school means attendant would be entirely comfortable in both of these settings. The point was that these people were quite comfortable with that designation, whether made by themselves or by others.

If becoming ordinary is relatively straightforward for some, this chapter will focus on those who find themselves in a very different position: immigrants. These are people for whom being merely ordinary was certainly not something they ever could have taken for granted and who may have good reason to struggle toward their occupancy of this category, people for whom being ordinary radically changes their relationship to British society more generally. Such a focus seems more than reasonable given a situation in which two-thirds of the participants in this study turned out not to be British in origin. We never chose to emphasis immigration; it was merely that the quiet cul-de-sac location of these streets seems to have appealed to a largely immigrant population. This is a global immigrant community from an extremely wide spectrum of locations; there is rarely more than a household or two from any single place of origin.

One problem with studies of migration is that it is assumed that migrants' aspirations are particular to their situation. Rather, we believe, the aspirations of migrants are the same as those of nonmigrants; it is just that they have a different starting point. So this chapter will also highlight the way the immigrant community helps make explicit and clarify an aspiration toward the ordinary that seems also to hold for most of the people in this study whose ancestry is British.

There is a vast literature on immigration and identity, and this in a way is precisely why academics have not appreciated the importance of being ordinary. The very word *identity* opposes itself to the ordinary. This literature has generally assumed that immigrants are faced by a decision: whether to identify with the cultural codes and values of the place they have come from or with those of the host society in which they now live. In recent decades this has included the development and subsequent decline of the term *multiculturalism* (Parekh 2000; Taylor 2002), which has had a range of meanings, including identity as some kind of syncretic blend, versions of cultural code switching (analogous to language switching), and models of complementary identities. Multiculturalism has emerged as a public and political debate over whether policies should promote diversity or assimilation (Lewis 2007). These discussions developed in turn from earlier concerns that centered on issues of assimilation and difference, all of which presumed that an immigrant exists within a state of alternatives that impose choices (or, as critics have pointed out, often a lack of choices). However, it was long ago appreciated that identity is not simply a matter of choice and aspiration but often something imposed by the dominant community. These questions of identity become increasingly problematic in a city such as London; as Gilroy (1987, 2004) shows, the relationship between a host population and various migrant groups is dynamic and dialogic. Yet such is the array of migrant groups in London, both first and second generation, that the question of who one identifies with or against is growing ever more complex.

Arguments over the relative position of migrant groups can easily rest upon assumptions of cultural inferiority and superiority, competing claims to morality and values, or individuals being turned into tokens that represent something called "culture." These identity issues are also famous for causing disputes within families and within institutions. It is hardly surprising, then, that while academic and colloquial debate has developed around these difficult issues, the populations that were the subjects of these arguments have contrived an alternative scenario that allows them freedom from the burden of all such concerns. At least in some cases, they have come to an appreciation that their lives would become easier if they were able somehow to junk identity altogether. What if there was a situation in which there was no such host culture, there was no culture from which people have come from, there was no initial state of difference, no issue of superiority or inferiority of values or morality? What if there was some technique of neutral abstention from culture? What if instead there was an imagination of a global ecumene to which all people have an equal right and in which all have an equal stake, because it says nothing about them at all, makes no claims and creates no issues? What if people could literally become nondescript? If we follow this thread, then the concept of the ordinary is turned around 180 degrees. Instead of being a failure to be something special in life, something to be denigrated, it becomes instead a kind of utopian fantasy of global equality. At this point, it seems more reasonable to see the ordinary as something people might strive toward—not through strident activism or overt political egalitarianism, which seems anything but ordinary, and perhaps not even with any consciousness of what they are doing, but through quiet unobtrusive movements in the significance of objects. In this process (which is better understood in the tradition of material cultural studies), an individual merely blends into this global state of the ordinary so effectively that the state itself is unremarked upon.

It is not our contention that this state has been entirely achieved, that all immigrants desire it, or even that it is necessarily a good thing. Rather, we argue that blue jeans are one of the most important contemporary modes by which this state outside of identity has been objectified and that many immigrants spend at least some of their time using blue jeans to come closer to such a state. First, however, we intend to put this into a wider context that fairly treats the spectrum of views and approaches to jeans we encountered within migrant populations. We need to give voice and space to those who have quite contrary views and aspirations and for whom jeans do quite other things, such as representing a loss of cultural values. We must also include those immigrants who clearly feel that they adopt jeans only as a result of pressure to conform or assimilate. We shall also find that the ideal of the unobtrusive ordinary is, at least in today's world, not yet seen as an attribute of an equal, undifferentiated world. Ironically, it will transpire that this ideal of the ordinary is itself regarded as being to some degree specifically British—though a type of Britishness (and in particular Londonness) that is in the vanguard of progressive movements toward inclusivity, rather than a conservative cultural form that defends exclusivity, as was previously the case.

THE COMPARATIVE CONTEXT

We do not want to suggest that jeans cannot be or never were associated with issues of identity, loss of culture, or multiculturalism. We have found instances, usually among older participants, of those who firmly avowed their commitment to the traditional dress of their region of origin, which may include the wholesale rejection of jeans. Madhulika, a forty-two-year-old from a farming village in Gujerat, always prefers to wear a sari and feels more comfortable in one. Such individuals may see jeans as something being foisted upon them as an act of conformity. Another woman has almost identical views, saying, "I just want to step into a sari. I don't like wearing jeans." The exception to this is when she is out with her children, as they "prefer Mum with a jeans and a T-shirt, to go out. At that age they get easily embarrassed." A third woman says her husband likes her in a sari at home. "But if we go out shopping, he doesn't like saris. 'Why don't you wear trousers?' He says that if you go to India you have to be Indian and if you go to England you have to be English. You can be whatever you wanna be, but if you go to Tesco, you have to wear English clothing. That's what he says. And I say, 'Why? You just have to wear something you feel comfortable with.' And he says, 'People will look at you,' and I say, 'So what?'" It is evident she feels comfortable wearing her familiar clothing, while for her husband, becoming inconspicuous is paramount. For this older generation, who have such clear and explicit concerns about fitting in, there seems to be a general trend toward increased jeans wearing over time. As one woman noted, the pattern is evident when one goes to pick up children from school. In primary school there are many grandparents involved, and many of those wear a sari or shalwar kamiz. By secondary school, one is more likely to see parents on school visits rather than grandparents, and they mainly wear jeans.

Then there was also the case of an older Indian man who claimed, "I would think that people are looking at me and I am not really comfortable when that happens. A similar thing is Indian clothes. In India I would wear Indian clothes when there is some function or anything, but in England—I don't want to attract attention." The irony in this case is that this older man always wore pressed brown trousers and a white shirt that anyone who has ever been to India would recognize immediately as quintessentially Indian, in effect the uniform of Indian males.

If we look at these examples as a group, it seems reasonable to suggest that more elderly immigrants tended to see jeans in terms of these older debates about cultural identity. For such people, jeans are seen as a sign of conformity, and potentially as an oppressive instrument of subjugation to the dominant aesthetics of the host community.

Both this group and some younger people may explicitly associate jeans wearing with loss of culture, though on closer inspection this is not at all what might have been expected. These migrants don't use an expression such as "loss of culture" to refer to their situation; rather, it comes up when they are discussing their region of origin. When they visit their birthplace, they are shocked at the extent to which people there have taken to wearing jeans. It is possible that, as many studies have found, migrants look to their place of origin as an ongoing source of ethnicity or authenticity that they hope will not make the changes they themselves have made; they wish it to remain largely symbolic of the place and time they left. At the extreme, as in Olwig's (1993) study of St. Kitts, an island can be turned into little more than a performance of authenticity for tourists from its own diaspora. So a migrant bemoans the way Croatians in Croatia are just copying the West in their increased wearing of jeans, but the same person has no such qualms about wearing jeans in London.

While younger migrants rarely have a problem wearing jeans in general, they may designate certain occasions as appropriate for traditional dress. For South Asian females, the problem at such times was not usually wearing jeans per se so much as wearing anything figure-hugging. One young woman got flak from her relatives in Pakistan when she went there for a visit because they found her jeans too tight. It is also sometimes immigrants who are more concerned not to wear jeans to a religious service, whether in a church, temple, or mosque. They may also be the ones who, apart from weddings, will specify family gatherings as occasions when jeans may be less suitable. As noted in previous chapters, overall young women of South Asian background showed much more concern about the shape of their bodies and about getting jeans that helped show their body to advantage. These were far more prominent concerns and anxieties than any interest in more formal prescriptions about what they could or could not wear. What they want from jeans is the garment's supposed ability to give shape and height to their appearance.

Jeans may also form part of the strategies people adopt toward the explicit multiculturalism that is found in Britain. As we have noted, the rejection of jeans as a sign of conformity is mainly confined to a few more elderly migrants. Much more common is the direct utilization of the way jeans, as the post-semiotic garment, can be said to go with anything. The classic example of this is the jeans worn to replace the shalwar or churidar of South Asian traditional dress but combined with a long kamiz or tunic that hides the degree to which tight jeans would show off the contours of the body. In the case of the churidar these were in any case often pretty tight to the legs prior to the adoption of jeans. We have previously discussed this combination of jeans and tunic as a solution to the impropriety of body-hugging dress in religious contexts, such as the mosque, but now we can generalize this to the idea that wearing an outfit that is a combination of what is seen as ethnic dress and non-ethnic dress resolves a more basic search for an expression of multicultural identity in the public domain.

All the above cases would suggest that jeans feature strongly in familiar arguments about multiculturalism and identity. But such cases are not typical of our research material on immigrants; when they do occur, it is mainly in the context of particular occasions such as family gatherings. We found far more evidence that leads us toward an alternative use of jeans as transcending such identity marking. The background to this is the perception of jeans in people's country of origin. Many of those we interviewed spent enough of their childhood in another country to have a strong idea of what jeans wearing meant at that time and in that place. These stories vary considerably. There were those who recalled a childhood entirely without jeans; a woman from Barbados associated this with poverty. Quite common are variations on an observation that Ivana makes with regard to Kosovo: that decades ago the area was more distinctive partly in that jeans were worn less often, but just as people in London have become more used to wearing jeans , so during the same period have people in Kosovo. So the distinction between the two areas has decreased. Asian families, even if they are not undertaking many return visits, have noted the dramatic increase in the incidence of blue jeans in Bollywood films; as Wilkinson-Weber (2011) has recently written, this has spurred the development of internal markets for denim in South Asia. Indeed, Arvind Mills in Gujerat was recently one of the top four denim producers in the world (see also Miller 2011). They therefore see the development of jeans wearing as a global phenomenon that would have happened to them even if they had not migrated to London. Satellite television channels such as Zee TV have carried pretty much the same message for South Asian migrants.

Sometimes informants go further and focus upon some other place abroad as better than the United Kingdom either in the quality of the jeans or in the way people there wear them. Three participants compare London unfavorably with the United States in terms of jeans wearing. One claims the United States has many more styles, more individual attention to personal style, and less copying than is the case with jeans in the United Kingdom. One prefers the way people wear jeans in France and remarks that her French husband always buys his jeans there. And we will introduce later in this chapter a Somali migrant with a very marked preference for Italian denim. On the other hand, one person we interviewed said British jeans were superior in style to those of Denmark. A common point of comparison was price, and this was almost the only reason anyone gave for continuing to buy jeans in their country of origin, such as Ecuador or Turkey.

Several participants particularly associated jeans with traveling. Miller has made this central to an essay on jeans wearing in Kannur, in the southern Indian state of Kerala (Miller 2011). This is a town in which there is a general resistance to the idea of mature males or married females wearing jeans, as it is perceived as a threat to traditional cultural values. But this went hand in hand with almost an insistence that jeans should be worn for travel. We found this idea among other people in our London research, including individuals from the Middle East and Southeast Asia, suggesting that this is one of the ways people express the idea of jeans having a relation to the global ecumene. Jeans thereby become directly associated with the placelessness or nonplace that Augé (1995) has associated with travel.

All of this is evidence that jeans are understood in relation to a sense of the global, rather than being considered particularly British in any respect. There is a universal conception of jeans now as a ubiquitous garment that can be found anywhere in the world; they are also associated with the cosmopolitanism of travel and transnational life. As a result, we can state clearly that there is no necessary assumption that coming to London and wearing jeans represents some kind of Westernization. We recorded a lovely story in this regard from Razan, who was brought up in urban Pakistan with short hair and wearing jeans. When she came to London and was sent to school, the authorities there failed to understand the implications of her name and assumed she was a boy. They simply didn't expect this level of sartorial gender equality in Pakistan. For several months she was too shy to contradict this and used the boys' lavatory.

Immigrants often claimed that jeans wearing was just as common today in their country of origin as in London. Often they noted that the particular style of jeans wearing was different, but this was viewed a product of fashion rather than cultural distinction. Participants talked, for example, about how Portuguese schoolkids all wore a version of sporty jeans, or a childhood in Malaysia where the main fashions followed from the film *Grease*. None of this fits with the idea that jeans wearing will increase as a direct result of migratory adaptation or assimilation. If, in practice, a move to London represents a shift from one style of jeans, such as sporty jeans, to another, such as boot-cut, no one would see this as expressing anything much about either location.

Indeed, it was almost as likely that the movement to London could be regarded as resulting in a decline in the quality if not the quantity of jeans wearing. A striking example of this perspective came from a woman who had migrated from Somalia. Previously her father used to work intermittently in Italy and brought her back what she recognized as very high-quality and well-fitting jeans. When she came to London she felt that everything was generally of a lower quality and that she had come to live in a generally inferior and less sophisticated country, at least with respect to jeans. By contrast, a man from Kosovo identified the United Kingdom, rather than the United States, as the source of the world's best-quality Levi's, something he clearly aspired to wear. It might not be wise to read too much into this last case, since we might surmise that people who come to the United Kingdom as their preferred destination for settlement are likely to be those who previously associated the country with high quality or other positive attributes.

BECOMING ORDINARY

In fact, apart from a short period in the 1970s based around Lee Cooper and Carnaby Street, there never was any particular association between jeans and being British. In order for jeans to become post-semiotic, they had first to slough off their association with the United States. What makes jeans ideal as an instrument for effectively leapfrogging any issues of the national and joining directly to the world at the transcendent level of the universal and the global is the fact that jeans are manifestly not seen by most migrants as an acknowledgment of any subservient position to the host culture. If a migrant assertively claims that jeans are worn just as much back in his or her country of origin, this is most likely a claim to equality of modernity in a very general sense. For most migrants, and most certainly for the children of migrants, wearing jeans is not an experience that can be reduced to issues of adoption of customs, a pressure to conform, or an explicit ideal of syncretic multiculturalism.

Many of these migrants originally came to the United Kingdom for some form of college education and found that college was exactly the kind of environment that favored ordinariness over multiculturalism. No one seemed to espouse an identity of difference or recognition; instead, they shared a general antipathy to conspicuousness in appearance. Students learned not only their material in their academic courses but also how to dress in a sort of generally scruffy way in which they only thing that was rendered conspicuous was an affectation to not care about clothing. This was most conveniently objectified in well-worn jeans. Such behavior often flew in the teeth of the initial assumption by their parents that the proper response of migrants should be the rapid adoption of respectability, as it had been for older generations. Parents sometimes reacted in horror to the "just got out of bed" look being cultivated by their children. Again, it was often the parents who retained the idea that brands should matter and that they constituted a new kind of respectability; their children rejected this notion in favor of either entirely brandless jeans or cheap retail brands, first Gap and more recently Primark.

In this respect, migrants go through much the same processes that were recorded in the last chapter for everyone equally. As people often note in relation to such claims for homogenization, a person may still be designated as black or Indian when wearing blue jeans, but this will be despite, never because of, that sartorial commonality. This relationship to jeans in college was true whether or not the students were migrants. Similarly, if they were younger when they migrated or if they are children of migrants, they would adopt jeans as an ersatz school uniform in the same way as younger children who were not migrants, and as they become older they would adopt jeans as a kind of middling ordinariness in the same way as housewives or workers of British ancestry.

As we indicated in the last chapter, ordinariness may be seen by people as an intrinsic aspect either of jeans or of the person. For example, a migrant from Albania made no remarks about the relationship between Albania and the United Kingdom, though Albania is one of those regions that retains the potential for stigmatization. This person is just naturally unobtrusive. She describes herself as restrained, not very emotional, quite controlled, not wanting to wear anything eye-catching, preferring to remain comparatively unnoticed. Her house is very neat and ordered and exquisitely ordinary. Perhaps it is those who have most reason to struggle for ordinariness who end up as in some ways especially ordinary. However, this woman is not representative of the migrant population we surveyed; one doesn't have to be particularly bland to wear jeans, or more unobtrusive than others. A woman doesn't have to wear jeans from Marks & Spencer or men Levi 501s, though certainly they can adopt such strategies, which lead toward a kind of hyperordinariness that signifies the ordinary to a greater extent than other jeans.

Most people are merely ordinary rather than hyperordinary. The way migrants come to take jeans for granted largely involve comfort and the processes described in the last two chapters. An example may help. The reason jeans are blue is, of course, because of their original association with indigo dye. Once a major plant crop throughout the world (Balfour-Paul 1998), indigo had virtually ceased to be used in dyeing, though there is starting to be a revival today, thanks to its use in very expensive jeans that tend also to be fair trade and made from organically grown cotton. We discovered during the course of our interviews that Selina's family came from Sierra Leone and Gambia, and her mother now lives around the corner. We were delighted to find out on one of her regular visits to the street that Selina's mother was herself an indigo dyer—not something we had anticipated in our study of denim, but very welcome. She gave us wonderful descriptions of how she used to extract the dye from the plant and the various wax resist methods by which patterns were stamped on cloth. Selina herself met her husband in France, had one child in Sierra Leone, and then bore two in London. She goes to a local church and is polite with her neighbors. She retains her own associations with indigo dyeing: when young, she used to travel to Liberia to sell the cloth her mother had dyed. She still wears her special indigo clothing, such as wraparound skirts, to family occasions. She recently walked into Marks & Spencer and saw a set of clothes in indigo that made her feel quite homesick.

Jeans were very much in fashion in Selina's childhood, but they came to her as secondhand clothes from a generic West. In those days there was a desire to emulate the American connotation of jeans, which was mainly restricted to the Levi's label. But also there was a powerful legacy of colonialism from the United Kingdom that dominated young Sierra Leoneans' ideas of how they wanted to look. She can recall ordering denim skirts from the Littlewoods catalogue, the excitement when after a month and a half their catalogue choices arrived, and the disappointment when they didn't fit and had to be sent back. In those days jeans were worn especially on weekends, when they all "let their hair down." She originally came to England to study at secretarial college, and then started to wear jeans far more often. They helped her mix in with everyone else, and she learned to dress them up for going out at night. She would also buy denim skirts, jackets, and jeans to send back to her daughter in Sierra Leone. During one period of her life she wore brand-name jeans with particular labels; her children were younger teenagers, a phase when brands matter, and they wanted their mother to be seen in them. But then they relaxed, and she relaxed, and jeans simply became foundational wear for her children; one in particular wore jeans pretty constantly.

Today Selina buys her own jeans in the United States simply because they are cheaper. However, the main role jeans have in her life has nothing to do with her relationship to indigo and not even much to do with her relationship to her children. Rather, she comes across as a fairly typical informant with respect to the discussion of jeans as comfortable. The jeans she has a real attachment to and identifies with are the ones that she has worn for ten years and which have subsequently become soft, intimate, and personal. It's not just that they signify a state of relaxation; they genuinely contribute to her ability to feel relaxed. One senses also that they are part of the way she feels comfortable in a wider social sense as just another person living in this area.

Selina still retains her marked cultural identity for those occasions where this is appropriate, such as a family wedding. Her husband is a staunch Jehovah's Witness, and she does not wear jeans for church. But in her everyday life she is content to have lost any particular affiliation or identity, to be just a mother and wife with her own career and personality, and in other respects to have achieved a state of being merely ordinary. In this state, wearing jeans is not a statement about who she is, but a means by which she can dress without making any kind of statement about anything at all. For a migrant to have become comfortable in the sense of bringing together the physical and social meaning of jeans, as described in chapter 4, is not quite the same as someone else feeling comfortable, for in the migrant's case it was not just the jeans but the people who were previously marked. So becoming comfortable may be an important and effective means of becoming a post-semiotic person.

LONDON: ORDINARY AGAINST VULGAR

Our argument would be somewhat tidier if we could point to a clear global ecumene of the post-semiotic garment and post-semiotic people. But looked at more carefully and from the perspective of migrants, it turns out that the situation is a little bit more complicated. London isn't just post-identity; it has the conspicuous identity of being better at post-identity than anywhere else. Not only that, but there soon seep in ideals of cultural superiority and perhaps even civilization that suggest London is not quite so far removed from earlier distinctions as might have been hoped. This emerges when we return to the evidence for comparisons that people invariably make between their sense of themselves in London and in their own country of origin. It is particularly clear when people talk of their return visits to their family or homeland.

To put it crudely, migrants start to consider other regions, including their own place of origin, as vulgar compared to London. It may be implicit rather than explicit, but it is often there as a subtext. Take, for example, one woman's comparison of London and the Arab states of the Persian Gulf. In London, you can "go out wearing Asda jeans and Tesco jeans and you wouldn't worry. Nobody would ever say anything to you. But over there it's a big thing what you wear." There is more emphasis on designer clothing and what she calls "show." "There's a lot of competition. Even the teachers in school would be dressed from top to bottom in Gucci." She contrasts this with London: "Over here I'm in my slippers and I'd run out of the house to drop my kids at school because I don't care what people think. I'm not bothered. But over there you just cannot leave the house until you have your makeup on and you're all dressed. I feel really fake and I just can't do that." She is adamant she won't change in the two years she and her husband will be living there for his job. They have recently been on a two-week trip to meet her husband's future colleagues, and she recalls that their wives and everybody else were "snobby and fake." In particular, she disliked the colors of clothing: "Shocking pink, the bright yellow and bright orange, and I say, 'Can I have light pink and pastel and navy blue?' They then say, 'But these are English colors. Why do you want English colors?' They resent that. They say, 'Oh no, we want to wear these because we live in a sunny place and everything has to be very bright.'" She contrasts this to her own preferences for wearing white or pastel colors in a hot climate. She never wears bright colors in London, but "when I go back there, because everybody's wearing it and that's all you find in the market, you end up picking one, and then you have that in your wardrobe, in your suitcase, and you say, 'Oh my God, did I really wear this?' You can't wear it. You can't think of wearing those colors."

There were many versions of these sentiments. Another woman tells us of trips back to Bangladesh, where people comment on her clothing as "a little boring, more like a schoolteacher outfit. They like bright colors. They follow fashion trends and design." She also sees the capital, Dhaka, as a place more concerned with fashion than London is. In reference to Pakistan, another participant notes, "Yes, it's changed a lot. They would know even more than us over there. They wear a lot of imitations, but they do go for the brands. It's always Diesel or Levi's. But they do wear a lot of fakes there, made locally." Similar remarks were made of Tanzania, Malaysia, Eastern Europe, and other regions. In these contrasts between London and a range of places throughout the world, the other places are characterized as interested in fashion, brands, and often brighter colors, whereas the muted, no-effort look of London is one that they feel happier with and more comfortable in. Some do talk, however, of changing their clothes when they go to another country in order to "fit in."

Clearly people in those regions see that the style of clothing that their relatives have adopted in London and continue to wear when they return home as drab and boring. Miller recalls one of his postgraduate students shocking her relatives with her grungy London jeans and lack of makeup. Her relatives were determined to "rescue" her and bring her home for a sartorial makeover. But these Londoners in turn have become defensive, and they advocate for this ordinariness as against having to be concerned with fashion, brands, or status competition, or indeed concerned about clothing at all. But one can also detect a sense of superiority against what is now seen as the vulgarity of brands and bright colors, perhaps even a feeling that other places are to that degree less civilized or at least less sophisticated.

This can also extend to comparisons made within Britain. One West African noted how she differentiated herself from Nigerians, who were much more dressy, "and you were wondering, are they going to a wedding or a top job or something?" Jeans were seen as negating the need for such clothing since they could always be dressed up when occasion demanded. Similarly, ordinariness in this sense might be specifically identified with London: people from other parts of the United Kingdom were said to be more concerned with makeup and accessories as opposed to the student grunge of London, with their "just got out of bed" hair and scruffy jeans. This view could equally well come from immigrants and nonimmigrants, though it can also be taken as a British rather than specifically London trait, linked with the kind of British affectation toward self-effacement described by Fox (2005) in *Watching the English*.

All of this shows that it would be a mistake to think that being post-semiotic is the same as being unmarked by others. Just as one can only signify becoming immaterial through some material signifier (Miller 2005), so also one can only look post-semiotic through some color or form that stands for that state of nothingness.* After all, being ordinary might be represented by bright yellow if everyone else is wearing it. People constantly forget that indigo is indeed a color—quite a marked color when on another garment—and that "pale" and "drab" are also colors in a sense. In a place where everyone else is striving to be in fashion and wears brands or designer clothing, not wearing brands or fashion is in fact a way of dressing extraordinarily.

A stance toward the ordinary that eschews these marked clothes and, within its own terms, is inclusive and avoids claims of moral superiority still comes across as a claim to moral superiority in relation to those who are not yet aspiring to be ordinary. This may be expressed by the idea that people in other countries still don't yet really "get it," that they have failed so far to engage with the potential of jeans for transcending such concerns. But these points work only within the context of transnational comparisons. Within the United Kingdom this takes on a more

---

* Which is why in an earlier footnote we admitted that technically post-semiotic is a contradiction in terms.

ecumenical dimension, as it loses most claims to particularity and makes no moral claims to superiority or being comparatively civilized. Its significance, at least within London, is that jeans have become the repudiation of all such presumptions.

Which leads to an important question of whether this global ecumene, if London is indeed in its vanguard, is in part a result of the capital's high percentage of migrants. There are good grounds for answering in the affirmative. London is in some ways a unique city, partly as a result of politics and partly because of demography. Politically it was dominated for quite some time by the figure of Ken Livingstone, first as leader of the Greater London Council from 1981 until 1986 and later as its first elected mayor, from 2000 to 2008. He led a systematic campaign over several decades to develop a positive image of multiculturalism. As this chapter has demonstrated, multiculturalism is quite different from the post-semiotic category occupied by jeans. Rather than being drab, pastel, nondescript, and indigo, Livingstone's multiculturalism was supposed to be a vibrant rainbow based on the retention of and respect for cultural difference.

If examined more closely, London's multiculturalism is a complex animal. It invokes a spirit of marked cultural difference, but only with respect to the aspects of a person's life that have now been designated as "culture," such as religion, the arts, and especially music. In London there are specific celebrations of culture, as in Carnival, a parade, or a *mela*. Beneath this is the foundational political universalism that avows the spirit of equality in opportunity and treatment. So the politics of the Greater London Council as fostered by Livingstone, with its constant sensitivity to racism, has tried to reduce any distinctions in education and other public domains while retaining certain specially marked niches for culture such as festivals and foods. What this politics has achieved is a more general assault on discrimination, contradicting its basic universalism. So Londoners were encouraged to retain ethnic clothing for marked occasions, or to be tolerant of those who wish to affirm specific forms of identity, such as young Muslims sporting fashionable hijab (Tarlo 2010). But beyond those marked images, London has promulgated the conditions of general equality or non-differentiation, best objectified in jeans. This is not to suggest it has entirely succeeded. It would obviously be naive to suggest that wearing jeans can in itself have the capacity to prevent any form of racism. It would equally be overly cynical and contrary to our evidence to deny that jeans have been able to signify an ecumenism that is not subject to such discrimination.

This politics achieved its most powerful translation in demography, which is what makes London fundamentally different from other cosmopolitan cites such as New York. London is unique in the extraordinary dispersal of ethnic concentrations across the breadth of the city before they could form ghettolike concentrations (Johnston, Forrest, and Poulsen 2002; Peach 1996; Simpson 2007). Ethnic populations that seemed to be concentrating in certain areas, such as Caribbean migrants in Brixton or Asian migrants in Southall, have since dispersed, as has historically been the tradition for the waves of migrants who occupied the East End, but only for a time. The streets we chose for our research are slightly unusual in this respect, as around a quarter of our participant population is of South Asian descent. This was unlike Miller's previous street ethnographies (2008, 1998), where there were no particular places of origin, just a completely diffuse pattern of settlement. As noted on several occasions already in this book, even this South Asian population is extraordinarily diverse, ranging from Muslim Pakistanis, Punjabi Sikhs, and Hindu Indians to Buddhist Sri Lankans. These people are as likely to see each other as threats as they are to see each other as comrades. So to say that there is a concentration of people of South Asian origin is no more significant than saying there are migrants from different parts of Europe on the same street. In our study area, migrants are represented by a smattering households from a wide variety of areas, ranging from Eastern Europe to South America, Africa to China. This again favors the kind of ecumenical cosmopolitanism that we see in jeans.

So London turns out to be highly relevant to this ability of jeans to become a kind of post-identity. In other studies, Miller (2008) has come across migrants who are quite explicit that they choose London to live in because they don't particularly identify with or want to be identified with the place they were brought up in, whether Brazil or Denmark. Surprisingly, there turn out to be quite a few people who don't particularly like the place they happen to have been born in, and are happy to repudiate that cultural identity. For them, being in London is perfect. But they don't want to exchange this for an identification with being British or even a Londoner. The attraction of living in London in a street with people from twenty other countries of origin is that they can become no one in particular, which is, as far as they are concerned, tantamount to being able to be themselves.

This is clearly important both in understanding the wider context of our argument and also in determining the degree to which we can and should generalize from our conclusions. The argument is not just that London may have become "nowhere" but that it has become "nowhere in particular"—that is, a site that is particularly good at standing for nowhere. This is not just our supposition; the evidence from demography and dispersal of populations suggests some objective measure of this attribute. But if London is particular in being so nondescript, then by definition it cannot be typical of anywhere. It is entirely possible that there is no other major city in the world that currently exhibits this pattern to the same degree. In that case, London is the ideal location for jeans to become post-semiotic with regard to identity, and we should be cautious in generalizing from it. Having said that, we believe London may be in the vanguard. Most major metropolitan cities exhibit some of this potential and are likely in the future to move closer to this state of becoming a place of nowhere that allows its inhabitants the possibility of repudiating as well as reestablishing any particular form of identity.

We simply don't have the evidence to be able to pronounce with authority on any of these possibilities. The discussions within this book derive merely from our study of blue jeans on these three streets; we may generalize to London, but any generalization beyond that would be speculative. Obviously we will be delighted if the ideas put forward here stimulate further comparative ethnographic study of other places and other forms of material culture, since the issue of typicality is obviously of considerable interest with respect to our claims about blue jeans, our claims about London, and our claims about the implications for immigrants. But for now we feel obliged to pause prior to any such comparisons.

CONCLUSION

This chapter started with examples that serve as caveats to any glib overgeneralization. There are people on these streets who feel burdened by a pressure to adopt jeans, which signifies a loss of their own traditions. There are others who see jeans as a direct expression of multicultural identity—they can match jeans with tops or accessories that identify them ethnically, but not too much, because they are wearing jeans. Some may also wear jeans of a type or in a manner that bears more on their relationship to friends and relatives in some other region, who may see jeans in that region as either superior or inferior to jeans as found in London.

Far more common than any of these are those who use jeans to opt out from any particularly affinity with identity. They may confirm to or even perform specific identities in what they see as appropriate contexts, such as family gatherings or religious assemblages, but they want to be able to step out of those associations for all other aspects of their daily lives. It is this capacity for a day-to-day existence without the burden of identity that we have emphasized. People who feel that even if this is not a state they achieve entirely, since they have no control over how other people may choose to designate or treat them, nevertheless see jeans as a positive gesture toward that aim. The post-semiotic property of jeans lends itself to the ideal of post-identity, which is to become no one in particular. Nowhere have we meant to imply that jeans in and of themselves can put an end to such identity or identification. A black or Asian individual in jeans will still be just as identifiable as black or Asian by his or her physical attributes. How far the lack of semiosis in the way that person clothes his or her legs has any bearing of the rest of this identification we cannot say. The argument is merely that in and of themselves, jeans can accomplish this task with respect to that particular part of a person's clothing, no more and no less.

The emphasis in this chapter has been on the migrant population because, as in the case of Selina, we can trace the various stages by which this trajectory has been realized. We can see why and how there might be a particular aspiration toward ordinariness, because the alternative was often inferiority or stigma. While this may be the case, it is also clear that in following such a path migrants simply make more explicit a trajectory that is equally true for those who are not migrants. The point they are heading toward is a point of aspiration for nearly the entire population, or at least for the Londoners who tend to live on such ordinary streets.

To have found a medium, jeans, that is genuinely transcendent and poses no possibility of inequality is not an achievement that should be scoffed at or dismissed as insignificant. The evidence in this chapter is that clothing can of itself be a medium for achieving political goals such as equality. On the one hand this may seem relatively insignificant being less politically explicit. On the other hand the intimate nature of clothing means that this is an achievement that can come to literally "feel right." People can feel better about themselves and more comfortable in public because denim gives a limited but genuine capacity to feel equal, to feel included through feeling merely ordinary.

Other aspects of this political goal of inclusive equality through being merely ordinary may prove far more difficult to accomplish, partly because they are more overt. But it has been an argument throughout this book, and indeed of material culture studies more generally, that just because something does not seem particularly deliberate or conscious does not make it less significant. If in the end we can only say that most people probably feel a good deal more relaxed thanks to blue jeans that is not something to take lightly. But this is perhaps a good point to leave the street, the relative parochialism of ethnography, and the circumspection of an analysis that is careful not to make claims beyond the limits of clear evidence. In the final two chapters we will embrace a much more ambitious agenda that looks to the implications for social science more broadly of the arguments we have made so far. How can what we have seen help us understand the nature of humanity and society in general?

CHAPTER 7

Anthropology

From Normative to Ordinary

The reputation of social science in the wider world has undoubtedly been tarnished over the last several decades by the public perception that much research makes claims that either seem entirely obvious to most people or produce original, perhaps curious results and information without making it at all clear why these matter sufficiently to anyone for time and money to have been spent obtaining them. Another way of putting this was the question we posed at the end of chapter 5: so what? We honestly do believe that prior to this research no one could give us a decent explanation of why people wear blue jeans. Our first task was to show that the usual functional, historical, and commercial reasons given don't really provide sufficient grounds. Given that jeans are what most people wear most of the time, then it is an important thing to explain in and of itself. So clearly this is not the kind of research that merely replicates an answer that most people, either jeans wearers or academics, can claim they were already well aware of. But now we think we have quite a few good answers.

What the last chapter added was the sense that this research is justified for another reason: that jeans really do matter to the people that we study. In fact, this has been clear from the very beginning of this book, because the anxieties that people face daily in deciding what to wear and what other people will think about how they dress cannot be dismissed as superficial if they can "ruin" that day for the individual in question. Jeans really may make the difference between feeling self-confident and able to cope with life or feeling as though one just wants to go home and hide under the covers. Neither of us would regard this as any less important because it is true more for women than for men. To this is added an appreciation that jeans may be of particular significance to migrant communities: they achieve something most communities genuinely strive for, which is a place in the world that depends neither on them being pigeonholed as representatives of the places they have come from nor on having to take on the mantle of the host society that they have moved to. Jeans can create that level playing field, one that relieves them of the burden of identity, at least with regard to one particular facet of appearance. As we have said, this is only clothing, and it does not stop someone from being categorized and denigrated in other respects, but that doesn't render it insignificant, either.

This research brings us an understanding that does seem important—it is not merely one more barb to add to some overstretched critique of society. We are empathetically engaging with something that populations have figured out for themselves as a positive strategy in coming to terms with modern life. This is also the case with our theory of global denim (Miller and Woodward 2011), which is that, as the most globally ubiquitous and simultaneously the most intimate and personal of garments, blue jeans help resolve the increasing distance felt between the individual and the sheer scale of the modern world—a major cause of alienation.

But these are not claims that would have come from either questionnaires or focus groups. They emerge from the kind of evidence that could only be obtained from material culture studies based on ethnography, because people who wear blue jeans are not generally conscious that these are instruments in a struggle by which immigrant populations come to terms with living in another society. Similarly, the argument that they achieve their ends by becoming ordinary rather than, for example, multicultural is also something that would not have arisen from conversation, since it is not a conscious or deliberate strategy. In fact, the key conclusion from the last chapter is perhaps that it takes an artifact of material culture to most successfully engage in a strategy that also works best below the level of consciousness. It is a facet of what social scientists these days call practice.

In answer to question "so what," as academics in social science, we also have a responsibility to say why these results matter to wider thinking about social science. We care a great deal about what is at stake here intellectually in terms of the kinds of questions that social science grapples with. As we outlined in the introduction, this book is intended to exemplify material culture studies as a branch of social science that arises out of and is grounded in detailed empirical research, yet remains committed to using this to understand issues at the other extreme of generality, exemplified by philosophy.

These final two chapters will outline our intended contribution to this other project. In this chapter, the ordinary will be considered in relationship to the normative and the fundamental issue of how societies reproduce themselves. Although these are questions present in debates throughout the social sciences, they are particularly pertinent to the discipline of anthropology, and as such, this chapter will concern itself predominantly with anthropology. This will be widened out in the subsequent chapter, which will look at social sciences more widely, although with a particular emphasis upon sociology.

Anthropology is the comparative study of society, in which we recognize the extraordinary diversity of cultural practices—that people in Iceland have entirely different customs and beliefs than do people in Argentina—and seek to theorize this both in its diversity and in general terms. Fundamental to anthropology from its inception have been questions such as what society is, how society operates, and how it reproduces itself from generation to generation. Contemporary anthropology has come to recognize that the world does not actually comprise a whole series of discrete little units, called societies or cultures, that are entirely homogeneous within and heterogeneous without. This was the way earlier forms of the discipline tended to represent the world to itself. But it never was the case, and it certainly doesn't fit our contemporary world.

Nevertheless, it is possible to understand that a typical Argentinean is much more like most other Argentineans than like a typical or even atypical citizen of Iceland, and, at least in the case of Iceland, there is a degree of homogeneity. So we can still discuss this pattern of variance without exaggerating it or ignoring the caveats. Not surprisingly, anthropology has developed a whole series of theories and models to account for how societies work and reproduce. The most coherent and comprehensive of these were initially evolutionary, in thrall to Darwinian discoveries in the nineteenth century, and then functionalist in the early twentieth century. Since then we have had various versions of structuralism, Marxism, theories of practice, postmodernism, and others. We are not about to engage with such theories. Instead we want to excavate still deeper, to a level that seems almost beneath the consciousness of most practicing anthropologists. We suggest that there exists an underlying conception that has been compatible with all these theories, a rather less explicit but for that reason perhaps even more fundamental assumption. This is encompassed by the term *normative,* and we highlight it here because by the end of this chapter we will suggest that this is where the concept of the ordinary seems to be most profoundly important to social science: as something that can potentially challenge and replace the normative. Although there are overlaps between *ordinary* and *normative,* we will specifically here be considering the differences and the relationship between the two.

At this point, we will put our study of jeans to one side and come to the ordinary through a very different trajectory: a history of anthropological accounts of society. In this context, *normativity* means simply the expectation that actions within a social field are likely to be judged as right or wrong, appropriate or inappropriate, proper or transgressive. Such judgments imply norms into which populations are socialized (Eriksen 2001, 59). The implication is that in any given society when one person sees another's action, the first person doesn't merely register this as an observation but inevitably also makes some kind of judgment about that action against what he or she regards as "normal" or "proper" behavior. This is especially true if the person performing the action is regarded as a member of the same population as the person observing the action. Irrespective of whether we have a functional or evolutionary view about society, this seems a basic principle, one that would explain how societies in general attempt to keep at bay any major variations from their own sense of the normal. This may involve institutionalized norms leading to explicit sanction. The action may be in breach of religious beliefs or legal requirements, or it may be seen as contravening what is regarded as "our customs."

The normative, as a facet of social practice, has no point of origin, in that it is hard to imagine any religion or moral order to which the normative has not been in some sense central. But when it comes to the more abstract or philosophical discourse around the concept of the normative, anthropology has been influenced by a tradition that derives in some measure from the writings of the philosopher Immanuel Kant.[*]

---

[*] While certain works by Stephen Turner are referred to in this chapter, we do not engage with Turner's much more detailed and systematic consideration of normativity in his recent book *Explaining the Normative* (Turner 2010). This is because that work is a highly erudite study in philosophy whose target is normativity as a position within academic

It is perhaps unfortunate that Kant wrote a book called *Anthropology from a Pragmatic Point of View* (2006). This book, the most popular of his works in his day, is today considered somewhat trite and among his least effective philosophical endeavors. The claim that Kant had a major influence on the discipline comes from elsewhere in his corpus (e.g., Kant 1999). It is Kant's, and more generally the Enlightenment's, understanding of morality as based on reason that became central to anthropological work. For Kant, moral order is normative, and not just by virtue of constraint and the obligations of duty. Moral action will follow when people act rationally given the particularities of the situation in which they find themselves.

This philosophical position has the effect of elevating the idea of the normative beyond that of "mere" custom. It links it with ideals of rationality and reason. This means that even societies that self-designate as modern, seeing themselves as repudiating mere custom or what they regard as irrational belief systems, will become just as dependent upon the normative as those societies they see themselves as replacing. But there is a problem here for anthropologists, because there is a clear opposition between this ideal of the normative as customary and the Kantian conception of normativity based on reason.

So the normative that is bequeathed to anthropology did not come directly from Kant, but was reconfigured through major foundational figures such as Emile Durkheim for the development of anthropology in Europe and Franz Boas for its development in North America. Gregory Schrempp suggests that "Kantian philosophy figured centrally in the perspectives of both Boas and Durkheim" (1989, 28; see also Turner 2010, 54, 123). The problem was that Kant's vision was universalistic, while anthropology needed a vision that respected cultural difference. Durkheim (1976) saw the social manifested as history prior to the individual. The social, then, becomes the a priori form through which systems of categories are realized analogous to Kant's use of the a priori in understanding how human beings experience the world. Boas, meanwhile,

---

philosophy. We are certainly sympathetic to its support of social science and in particular to the turn back to empathy in its final chapter as a means of escaping what he regards as the circularity within philosophical normativity. But we don't feel qualified to engage at this level of philosophical debate and are more comfortable with what we see as largely colloquial and anthropological uses of the term *normative* as it is employed here, which certainly lack the rigor of his investigation. For anyone wanting to go deeper into the presuppositions and implications of the normative, Turner's book would seem essential reading.

takes on more of Kant's ideals of scientific exploration and envisions a separate cosmological sphere that transcends science. Both of them seem torn between the study of society as the particular and Kant's universalism.

As anthropology developed into a recognizable discipline within its own norms, it increasingly relied on a concept of culture that was influenced by many other writers, including Edward B. Tylor and Johann Gottfried von Herder. This concept of culture starts to open up what appears to be an irreconcilable difference between anthropology and Kantian philosophy. For Kant, the vision of anthropology is simultaneously individual and universal. The idea of reason implies a direct link between the two, as each individual carries within him- or herself the potential for a universal and cosmopolitan morality. This link was sundered by the anthropological discovery of cultural relativism. For anthropologists, the world is organized not by universal reason but by the much more parochial vision of cultural values specific to different populations. This view effects a repudiation of universalism through an alternative emphasis on a collective that is bigger than the individual but smaller than the universal.

Nevertheless, anthropology retains something of the Kantian ideal in its presumption of the normative as the ruling principle that exists within each and every cultural vision. Anthropologists, in the main, assume that all people have, as Kant argues, an essentially moral vision of the world linked to reason but that this vision takes shape within each specific cultural context rather than within a universal humanity. An appreciation of the mindless killings in the trenches of the First World War at least muted any simple assertion of the moral superiority of the civilized West. In particular, a tradition from Boas through Melville Herskovits developed a powerful normative relativism based on the commitment not to judge other peoples by one's own moral viewpoints but to appreciate that they will see themselves in terms of their own situated logic. This relativism between populations was also implicated in a concept of culture that supposed that, within a given population, people did judge each other according to a normative framework that was not, for them, relativistic. So the anthropologist as ethnographer is faced with at least some of the same questions posed by Kant about how a population creates either consensual or imposed moral judgments, at least with respect to intracultural behavior.

As noted above, contemporary anthropology allows for much more diffuse ideas of society that eschew the degree of homogeneity presumed by these earlier theories, but the basic idea of a normative order within a world of cultural relativism has remained. Not all anthropology is besotted by cultural relativism. In some instances, the discipline retains a clear predilection toward its own moralism. Some anthropologists also assert that we can and should distinguish between universal and particular moralisms (e.g., Merry 2001; Scheper-Hughes 1995). In general, though, anthropologists mostly subscribe to a Kantian vision when taking an intracultural view, but not when it comes to the pluralities of cultures other than our own, toward which we may feel obligated to abstain from moral judgment. Within such cultural relativism, it seems that Kant's anthropology cannot be our anthropology. As we argue below, however, new developments around the concept of the ordinary may lead to a potential rapprochement.

As anthropology became more committed to the minutiae of ethnographic particularism and the explanation of social order, the normative became increasingly an implicit assumption rather than the source of a general theory. Within some subfields of anthropology normativity has remained relatively explicit, while in others it has become increasingly implicit. The normative foundation for culture is clearest in fields such as the anthropology of religion and the anthropology of law. But in other genres of anthropology, norms are often derived from statements about organizational principles. So kinship theory, as a core to anthropological studies, is not just a system of categories by which people recognize their relationship to each other. It also specifies the forms of behavior expected of individuals who occupy a given relationship, such as a mother's brother or a sister's son, and thereby incorporates normativity. Within economic anthropology, to cite another example, we teach about the disputes between approaches we call formalism and substantivism, but in effect what is at issue is whether one regards a single set of economic principles as pertaining to all peoples or subscribes to an alternative, more relativistic sense of situated economic expectations. Either way, the assumption is that these positions represent norms and principles by which actors are judged and disciplined. More or less the same argument goes for any other branch of anthropological investigation; at root, they all assume normativity.

An assumption of local normativity is thus the other side of the coin to cultural relativism. Anthropology remains committed to empathetically engaging with an extraordinary diversity of practices, from derivatives trading to cannibalism, and with vast mythic structures. This engagement is achieved by trying to comprehend the incredibly wide range of moral universes in terms of their own normativity, such that inside any given system of values are expectations of and constraints on individual action. The first thing an anthropology student is usually taught is that although any given set of observable behaviors of another society might at first appear bizarre relative to the expectations and beliefs of the student's upbringing (an example would be the "menstruating men" of New Guinea's Wogeo people, described in Hogbin 1970), these behaviors would be regarded as moral duties within the society being investigated. It is the outsiders' refusal to countenance such actions that would be seen as bizarre by that population.

The high point in the study of culture within this relativist tradition may well be the work of Clifford Geertz, who stayed close to these questions of normativity to the end of his career. His immediate concerns had originally been more the repudiation of the functionalist paradigm that preceded him, with what he regarded as its simplistic and mechanistic assumptions about the normative. As he notes in *Available Light,* for functional analysis, "'religion' holds society together, sustains values, maintains morale, keeps public conduct in order, mystifies power, rationalizes inequality, justifies unjust deserts, and so on" (Geertz 2000, 15). Without this functionalist concept of religion, there clearly needed to be something else to serve the normative. In his work, this tended to be shared frames of meaning, whose consequences were in some ways analogous to those of functionalism (the last chapter of *Available Light* is called "What Is a Culture if It Is Not a Consensus?"). More recently, anthropology has tended to disown the study of culture per se, as it has repudiated the idea of bounded and homogeneous cultures. But if instead the focus is on women, for example, or ethnicity, or subcultures, it is not clear how this does more than downsize the problem of culture as normative. If one undertakes an ethnography of an anti-state, ex-hippie radical collective, the result would still be the ethnography of a community structured around the normative values of anti-state, ex-hippie radicalism (see, e.g., Malaby 2009 on how technoliberationist ideals were put into practice through the creation of Second Life). Our concern here is not with the concept of "culture," which has spawned a huge literature, but with our belief that both "culture" and alternative constructs (such as "society" for the writ large, and "identity" or "resistance" for the writ small) imply a concept of the normative that has become increasingly taken for granted but remains fundamental.

This at least would have been the case with the traditional anthropological monograph that describes the patterns of behavior or custom in any given society and thereby implies that a person who failed to carry out a ritual that was appropriate for him or her, or who failed to make an exchange with another who occupied a particular kinship category relative to that person, would be subject to opprobrium if not actual sanction and punishment. To bring this up to date, however, we need to engage in a bit more detail with the new forms of anthropology that have developed in the last couple of decades. One of these has put far more emphasis on issues of power, having been influenced by the writings of Michel Foucault (see Rabinow 1999; for a critique, see Brown 1996). Other trends in anthropology have emphasized a heroic struggle against any given norm. Some anthropologists tend to celebrate critique, marginality, struggle, and resistance, as though all cultural norms are inherently oppressive and all heterogeneities are inherently liberating. This tendency ignores the equal desire by people who regard themselves as progressive to actually create and extend global norms. Examples in this vein are movements such as feminism and ideals of equal rights to power or welfare, which most anthropologists think of as generally a good thing. Notwithstanding debates within these areas over, for example, who defines the ideas and norms of feminism and whether these are fully inclusive, we do not assume that feminism is intrinsically oppressive and that every good anthropologist has, as a kind of birthright, a duty to resist the universalist moralities of feminism and refuse its constraints. The tension between advocacy of and opposition to norms is only partially resolved through various fashionable notions of heteronormativities or multiple ontologies. Stephen P. Turner (2010, 119–49) carefully dissects the assumptions of collectivity that underlie all such arguments.

A more satisfactory route, one that brings this excavation of normativity up to date, would take note of anthropologists' increasing reliance on a theory of practice.* For contemporary anthropologists who feel the need to make explicit their theoretical underpinnings, this is probably the most commonly favored theoretical agenda. Whereas with Geertz we still find a sense of a moral system of expectations, when we come to Bourdieu (1977), we confront something more like a banal

---

* The next few paragraphs on practice theory and normativity probably represent the most obscure and obtuse section within this volume as a whole. It is important for understanding contemporary anthropological theory, but possibly not essential to understanding why people wear blue jeans, so if you feel yourself drowning, skip lightly over the surface and rejoin us on the more familiar lands that lie ahead.

system of socialization through the engagement with embodied routines. In *Outline of a Theory of Practice*, Bourdieu developed his concept of habitus. He argued that people are socialized into being typical members of the society they live in not through explicit instruction but through embodied routines based on interaction with the material world around them, which itself is organized into specific patterns. Within a house, for example, we instinctively know what is supposed to be high or low, dark or light, at the front or at the back. And thereby we know where we should sit or stand, whether we should act formally or informally.

The emphasis on this minutiae of everyday material things as doing the heavy-duty work in socialization does not seem to require either religion or function, merely routine, but as Sherry B. Ortner (1984) noted, there is still a great deal to work out in terms of how practice contributes to social reproduction more generally. A starting point may be that "practice theories are motivated in substantial part by Wittgenstein's and Heidegger's criticism of normative regularism, which identified the understanding of norms or meanings with grasping and following rules" (Rouse 2007a, 668). But if people are not following rules, does this mean there is some underlying or implicit normativity that still explains why we do what we do?

The implications of a theory of practice for implicit normativity have recently been subject to heated debate within philosophy (Rouse 2007a, 2007b; Turner 2005, 2007; see also Honneth 1995; Zurn 2005). As Turner (2007, 66–67) notes, the problem with seeing something as merely given is that this seems to place it outside of causative explanation. For Turner, this is not acceptable. A key example is his discussion of anthropological debates concerning the Maori *hau*. *Hau* plays a role in one of the most hotly debated case studies within the entire discipline of anthropology. It derives from the work of Marcel Mauss, who theorized that a gift should be understood as a primary mechanism for the formation of social relations. If party A gives something to party B and party B then feels under some obligation to reciprocate that gift, then parties A and B are in a relation with each other. But where does this obligation to reciprocate the gift come from? The case study that Mauss used was taken from the Maori of New Zealand, who used the word *hau* to account for the necessity to return the gift.

Most readings suggest that *hau* is not merely a description of the practice of giving something back. For the Maori, *hau* is a causative explanation implying magical processes whose power comes from within the forest. But Mauss, says Turner, is in effect supplying an alternative, de-mystified account of *hau* as his contribution to social science, through his own explanation of its existence and consequences. Mauss's analysis confirms for Turner that, one way or another, people have to understand why they should do something. That is, either we propose that the Maori have to have reasons for their beliefs or Mauss has to propose an anthropological explanation for their existence. Otherwise, we do not feel we understand *hau*.

Our position, however, would be closer to that of Joseph Rouse (2007b, 47) in his critique of Turner.* Rouse argues first that we can retain an idea of implicated normativity within practice theory and, second, that this does not require the forms of explanation Turner insists on. For Rouse, the discussion of *hau* is exceptional rather than typical. Anthropologists, and quite possibly the Maori, explicitly debate *hau*, but most things are not like that. With regard to many observed social or individual actions, we do not assume that those engaged have necessarily developed a pseudo-causative account for those actions. More often, they merely regard their actions as customary, as routines, or as entirely obvious. If we do not presume that the Maori require a causative account of their actions, then perhaps we also may not need an alternative social science version, a "demystified" causative account based on an implicit normativity. In some ways, a theory of practice obviates each of these requirements.

Instead, actions may be regarded as an expression of the merely familiar that makes people in shared social processes feel comfortable. In London, eating your dessert before your main course is subject to normative pressure, not because anyone would regard it as immoral but because it would be judged as making those in the vicinity feel uncomfortable. It is possible that those involved could come up with an ad hoc folk explanation for their feelings of discomfort: perhaps eating a sweet before a savory dish might make you feel sick. It is also possible to come up with an account from social science. Following Mary Douglas (1978), we might regard the order of meals as symbolic of some deeper social order. But following Rouse, we do not have to presume either of these cases. Practice is merely socialized routine. Routine may, in turn, become subject to normative critique. Figures such as Theodor Adorno

---

* We are ignoring the wider context to this discussion that develops when Turner returns to the *hau* as part of his overall critique of the philosophical normativism (Turner 2010, 59–63).

and Henri Lefebvre (Slater 2009; Wilk 2009) railed against routine, especially the routines of contemporary consumer culture, as a betrayal of the kind of consciousness people should aspire to. It has taken quite some time for social science to empathetically engage with the study of routine in its own right (see Shove, Frank, and Wilk 2009).

Our stance aligns with this more relaxed attitude to social practice. We believe that most people are happy enough to stick to the normative within their own societies without feeling they constantly need to justify or legitimate every single action they take. The more routine those actions, they less they become subject to such scrutiny. Rather, as Gombrich (1979) says of art and Goffman (1975) of human behavior more generally, we are aware of these routines as frames of acceptable behavior only when someone breaks those frames and acts in an entirely unexpected manner, So within anthropology, thanks to the work of Ortner, Bourdieu, and many others, socialized and embodied routines are no longer seen as a static set of rulelike behaviors. We understand that they can incorporate considerable variation that provides much of the dynamic force to society. This variability is also what makes habitus compatible with social change. But we still need to understand how routine is linked to the normative. For Rouse (2007b, 53), social action as performance is normative because it is accountable by reference to a common stake in social expectations. So practice should not be seen just as regularity among people but as a "pattern of interaction among them that expresses their mutual normative accountability" (Rouse 2007a, 669). To put this simply, we have moved from the idea that people have to feel a sense of duty to the idea that they are sensitive to what makes other people feel comfortable.

So with Rouse, anthropologists have an argument that seems to bring our concept of normativity into alignment with the increasing preference for a theory of practice and, equally, with the particular approach to material culture studies with which we would wish our own work to be associated. This form of material culture studies has for a long time sought to distance itself from the more romantic elements of traditional anthropology that were, in some measure, partly responsible for an emphasis on the normative, especially in its earliest forms that stressed moral holism. The idea of material culture as representing "the humility of things" (Miller 1987) implied that objects as practice often tended to be below the radar of normative surveillance. Precisely because we don't see the color or type of curtain or the color or type of trousers as having the same authority as a piece of legislation or a religious command, we don't take such things as seriously when trying to understand why we do what we do. But if most of our behaviors are actually learned and enacted through the minutiae of the material things around us, then the fact that we don't take them seriously and therefore are less likely to challenge them may make them still more important in determining our actions. An example would be the way blue jeans act to help immigrant communities escape from the dilemma of having to choose to identify either with their place of origin or with the host society, the argument being that jeans are most effective in this role when no one is aware that this is happening.

To summarize, the argument has been that, almost irrespective of the dominant theory of the time, anthropology remains dependent upon an increasingly implicit assumption of normativity. At first the normative was best understood in terms of those areas where anthropologists recognized there would or could be some sense of opprobrium for non-normative behavior, that if it didn't break religious sanctions it would at least be said to contravene custom. In recent years, however, with the rise of practice theory, anthropologists have looked closely at much less obvious and more basic social orders found in the everyday world of material culture, within which people are socialized into those customs. While some philosophers assert that we must have an explanation that accounts for why we do what we do, others such as Rouse match this reliance on everyday trivial objects around us with an idea that while non-normative behavior merely makes us feel uncomfortable, that is enough for the normative to reemerge, since making other people feel uncomfortable is sufficient cause for normative responses—not just in the very mannered world of Jane Austen but also in our day-to-day life.

The appeal to discomfort has the fortunate consequence of giving us a point of reentry for the other trajectory we temporarily abandoned, that of blue jeans. Chapter 4 was devoted to precisely this concept, in terms of feeling comfortable and uncomfortable, and from within an ethnographic setting lends credence to Rouse's philosophical conjectures. But we now want to suggest that if chapter 4 seems to conform to these ideas about normativity, then chapter 5 represents a profound challenge to those same ideas. There are a whole slew of circumstances in which it seems reasonable to shelter jeans under the umbrella of normativity, especially when we have a starting point such as a woman being beaten up for having the temerity to wear them. Similarly normative was when jeans carried connotations of transgressive youth or when they were seen as inappropriate for particular types of people by age or class or background. When today at the workplace it is said to be inappropriate to wear jeans when serving the public, this too implies normativity, as does the feeling that they are inappropriate at a wedding.

While there are many conditions that continue to relate denim to the normative, the main trajectory of this volume has been toward an emphasis on denim as a kind of post-semiotic, post-identity garment. It was suggested in chapter 6 that the setting of our study, London, is highly relevant to this conclusion, as London has become the ideal place for people who don't want to be identified with anywhere in particular. Many migrants see this as one of the major advantages of living in London, with its unusual degree of ethnic dispersal. It offers a superior opportunity for escaping from identity. For example, when Miller recognized that a participant in an earlier project was from Brazil, he became interested in knowing about the aspects of the participant's life that pertain to that Brazilian identity. He embarked on conversations by asking him when and whether he eats Brazilian food or if he has Brazilian friends, to which the respondent answered, "If I wanted to be fucking Brazilian I would have stayed in fucking Brazil" (Miller 2008, 179–85).

The great advantage of London, with its combination of diversity and dispersal, is that when migrants decide to loosen an affinity with a place of origin, they do so not because they feel under pressure to identify with London itself or with being British, which they might feel if living in another part of the United Kingdom. After all, in the streets where we carried out this fieldwork, having one's origins in London is a minority position, not a majority one. To the chagrin of many more conservative or right-wing politicians, there is in the United Kingdom relatively little explicit valorization of a specific British or English identity, at least compared to identification with a local soccer team. Similarly, migrants may not feel anything but a remnant or token association with the place where they spent their childhood or where their parents were born. They may be bored and irritated by endless inquiries along the lines of "Where do you come from?" Many do indeed have a strong relationship with a place of origin, one that may grow even if they were born in the United Kingdom. But the growing tendency for many people is simply not to identify with identity.

In this struggle against identity, perhaps one of migrants' most valuable allies is denim blue jeans—not designer jeans or other special jeans, but the kind of jeans people buy from shops such as Asda and Primark and which correspond to what the people we quoted in chapter 3 refer to as "classic," "standard," or "proper" jeans. These are the jeans we refer to in chapter 4 as "post-semiotic," the ones that most of our informants wear most of the time they wear jeans. In chapter 5 we saw that such jeans have become a panacea against internal feelings of discomfort—they are the antacid of our clothing world. They help us avoid feeling uncomfortable in public under the gaze of others, or uncomfortable physically.

This leads to a crucial question about the relationship between the normative and the ordinary. If there is pressure in our society to wear blue jeans, to become merely ordinary, and if people feel a sense of opprobrium to the degree to which they fail to wear jeans or fail to be merely ordinary, then it would be reasonable to see the ordinary and its association with jeans as also settled within the embrace of the normative. It is not impossible for this to be the case. There were examples in the previous chapter of older migrants who felt that they needed to fit in or assimilate and saw the wearing of blue jeans as something that would be therefore expected of them. But from the perspective of our fieldwork as a whole, this is highly exceptional. Most migrants, and especially younger migrants, feel that if anything, the pressure is on them to represent some kind of identity (in contrast to the rest of the population), while wearing blue jeans represents some sort of escape from such questions. None of them ever reported that they were harassed for not wearing jeans. Quite the opposite—the pressure is to wear something special, symptomatic of the pressure to be someone special. To be merely ordinary is not usually an accepted ambition in life. It is hard to envisage a scene in which a parent turns to a child at the point of maturity and says, "My child, now that you are becoming an adult, what I really want for you is to achieve a state of ordinariness." Returning to the default mode of putting on everyday jeans or being content to be an ordinary person is inevitably reported as a means of opting out of all such pressures rather than conforming to them. For all these reasons, the ordinary stands against the normative.

As such, the ordinary achieves a position beyond that of moral inferiority or superiority, beyond conformity or distinction. It is no more moral than it is immoral. Moral evaluation is not an intrinsic property of being ordinary because ordinariness is subject to different consequences in different contexts. In London, the ordinary is something rather unprecedented. It cannot signify being a Londoner or being British because people in countries other than the United Kingdom wear jeans just as commonly. It does not necessarily signify gender, class, age, or indeed anything at all. The ordinary represents a kind of post-semiotic global ecumene, but we would be quite wrong to suggest that people wear jeans precisely to achieve some higher political or religious goal of global equality. That is effect, not cause. There is no sanction or discourse that makes it normative, even in the sense employed within practice theory. It is more a relaxation into the state of not wanting to be anything in particular, including not particularly ordinary.*

So denim jeans represent a fundamental break from the anthropological recourse to the normative in understanding society. They demonstrate the degree to which common practice can be achieved in ways other than by sanctions and pressures to conform, through a sense of or ambition toward duty, or even by the following of practice as routine. Rather, we can start from the position argued by Rouse (2007a, 2007b) with regard to a practice theory that does not require explicit or conscious explanation for itself. This will be explored further in the next chapter, as it is central to how and why the ordinary matters. Jeans are a form of material culture in which an ideal of the ordinary is objectified through people as material practice, rather than as the sign of those people's intentionality, duty, aspiration, or identity.

Jeans wearing cannot be assimilated within the implicit assumption of normativity that has been the foundation of anthropology for most

---

* As an aside, blue jeans do seem to correspond to a resolution of the initial conflict between Kant and anthropology. This was the contradiction that arose from cultural relativism. Blue jeans, as ordinary, do not express that cultural relativism. The ordinary emerges as in some ways a suppression of culture as difference. Rather, blue jeans return us to the initial linkage between the individual and the universal in Kant. Blue jeans dominate the world today partly because they are simultaneously the most personal and the most global garment a person can wear and, to that extent, help people resolve the growing gulf between the personal and the global. This ability of jeans is why we can both write this volume and edit a book on global denim (Miller and Woodward 2011) that looks ethnographically at the extraordinary range of denim in diverse cultural contexts.

Jeans as the ordinary seem to accord to at least one aspect of the Kantian ideal, beyond the tension that has always existed between anthropology and Kant, and indeed within Kantian philosophy itself (Frierson 2003; Kant 2006), though it cannot be reconciled with Kant's ideal of the categorical imperative or its separation from what he regarded as mere practical reason. We are not arguing that people wear blue jeans because they are conscious that in so doing they move forward an ethical imperative toward equality and universality. What people say is only that jeans make them feel comfortable. What Kant hoped would be achieved through moral consciousness is here achieved through largely unreflective material culture. It is through the blue jeans themselves that equality is objectified in the sense of that term as Miller derived it from Hegel (Miller 1987). It is also evidently not the act of enlightened self-consciousness of the kind that not only Kant but also Hegel and most Enlightenment thinkers saw as central to the progress of reason as a form of enlightenment.

of its history and which remains an implicit device even within theories of practice. Instead, this study of material culture leads to a quite innovative understanding of how and why people engage in actions that may become ethical in their consequences rather than through their intention. If jeans wearing is essentially an expression of people not wishing to make other people uncomfortable, then it would almost exactly correspond to Rouse's (2007a, 2007b) arguments for the implicit normativity of practice theory. That is to say, we could still ascribe moral intention to it. But our ethnography does not confirm Rouse's perspective either, because it suggests that comfort is more an expression of people's concern with themselves than of their regard for others. Jeans put the wearer at ease before they put others at ease. So our concluding emphasis is not on practice theory but on material culture. People do not wear jeans to express their desire for equality, yet, as material culture, jeans do in some small measure render people more equal. Wearing ordinary jeans is consequentially, not intentionally, moral, which is why we do not think it could be termed normative.

Wearing blue jeans obviously does not mean that class, income distinctions, gender, or any other distinctions have disappeared. There remains an endless supply of cultural difference and cultural sanctions for anthropology to study, and vast disparities in life's expectations for anthropologists to oppose. For those who wish to study the anthropology of power, identity, or resistance, the field remains wide open. Indeed, there is nothing in this book to contradict those who wish to argue that inequality is all the more invidious when it is hidden by implicit forms such as taken-for-granted clothes rather than expressed through overt signifiers of difference, though this is not our position. Such academics could then use the evidence presented here to argue that blue jeans exacerbate inequalities. By contrast, we would argue that the elimination of overt difference does in some small way contribute to a potential for equality in the contemporary world, and we would celebrate this global ecumene of jeans.

This chapter has been an attempt to exemplify the idea that grounded ethnography is not at the other end of the spectrum from philosophical generality but rather is perhaps the only safe place from which to engage in philosophy without being sucked into the ether of abstraction. The particular conundrum we have tackled is whether anthropology has any alternative to a dependence upon the normative in understanding society and social reproduction. We have argued that the concept of the ordinary as embodied in blue jeans corresponds to just such an alternative. While this may not of itself liberate the world or create global equality, it does at least represent a significant advance in anthropological theory. The objectification of the ordinary in jeans is a remarkable achievement, the kind we tend to ignore precisely to the degree that it is neither marked nor intended.

CHAPTER 8

Sociology

The Ordinary and the Routine

Chapter 6 established the significance of being ordinary to the people we studied, while chapter 7 examined the consequences of this for our understanding of how society reproduces itself and the challenge this represents for the concept of normativity as used in anthropology. By contrast, in this final chapter we recognize that to select denim as a topic of academic inquiry is to invoke another sense of *ordinary*, that is, quotidian and mundane. This gives rise to a quite separate debate about when, why, and how academics should turn their attention to what otherwise might seem more banal topics of inquiry, including denim. In addressing the question of why we should study denim, and the concomitant issue of why denim matters to the people who wear it, we are both echoing and also drawing upon debates in the social sciences more widely, including studies of the routine and the mundane.

Discussions of the routine and the ordinary have been of concern within various diverse strands of social science research, ranging from phenomenological approaches and microsociological theories of everyday life (spanning ethnomethodology up through writers such as Goffman) to more recent developments in practice theory (Shove, Trentmann, and Wilk, 2009). Ethnomethodological approaches have perhaps been the most explicit in addressing the question of what the ordinary is and how it is accomplished through mundane and reflexive actions. Within much of the rest of the literature on the mundane and the routine, ordinariness is implied but not fully explored. In this chapter we will examine more concretely how theories of the routine, especially when connected to the study of material culture, can help make apparent why the ordinary matters so much, both to the people we study and to theory in social science. There is often an elision between the concepts of the ordinary, social norms, and the term *everyday*, and it is the last that has gained perhaps the most attention within the social sciences, following from the writings of de Certeau and Lefebvre. While there is certainly an overlap between these terms, this chapter will argue that there is also something distinctive about a focus upon the ordinary.

We will start by considering the ways in which the ordinary has been theorized by writers such as Raymond Williams to try to understand what it is and how it is defined. We will then turn to a consideration of the ordinary through the lens of the routine and the mundane, as it is that sense of the ordinary that our ethnographic material speaks to, and which makes most apparent the larger importance of the concept, since it refers to what most people do most of the time. Finally, we will argue that theorists of the routine and of practice, such as Bourdieu and Giddens, lead us back toward a consideration of material culture as the medium through which to understand the ordinary as often unspoken practice and routine.

THE NEGLECT OF THE ORDINARY AND ITS MISAPPROPRIATION

Gronow and Warde (2001) offer an argument as to why sociology has not paid full attention to the mundane and what they term "ordinary consumption," as opposed to a focus in consumption studies on distinctions such as status and social divisions such as class. This claim certainly holds true for academic work on clothing, which tends to focus on fashion, designers, or spectacular, rarely worn items of clothing, rather than more humble and mundane garments. Even histories of jeans tend to be written in terms of movie stars such as James Dean and Marlon Brando. Within the wide range of literatures that deal with the sociology of everyday life, Sandywell has argued not only that explicit considerations of the ordinary have been neglected, but also that by being elided and concealed within this concept of the everyday, the ordinary is "denigrated" (2004, 161). This is in part why we feel it is important to theorize the ordinary. A focus on the ordinary may also seem at odds with current academic fashions within gender theory and wider social theory influenced by poststructuralism and postmodernism, which tend to emphasize fluidity, heterogeneity, and a lack of fixity. However, being ordinary is not necessarily in opposition to difference or heterogeneity, in that it does not necessarily imply homogeneity. Finally, there is also a methodological point regarding this lack of consideration of the ordinary. Many of what have emerged in this book as the most significant aspects of the relationship that people have to mundane clothing such as jeans are not normally verbalized but emerge only as practice. Therefore, the privileging of verbal accounts within sociology and the sovereignty of the interview is insufficient to grasp such relationships. Recent developments around practice theory and innovative methodological developments (such as Pink 2009) have started to grant us more access to the nonverbal within sociology.

Though there has been a lack of explicit focus upon the ordinary, it is at least implicated in many studies of the everyday. However, these have often been problematic. On one hand, there is a tradition within cultural studies, emerging from influential work by Richard Hoggart (1969) and Raymond Williams (1958), of paying attention to the ordinary and everyday, but at the cost of romanticizing the common man and ordinary life, especially in relation to a celebration of previously denigrated working-class culture. On the other hand, the ordinary and the everyday have been subject to relentless critique as merely manifesting the forces of capitalism and homogenization, as in writings by the Frankfurt School. These two tendencies come together in the work of de Certeau (1984) and Lefebvre (1991), each of whom, in his own way, regarded everyday life as something to be critiqued, while claiming to recognize some hidden potential for positive transformation or liberation. This is also reflected in the work of Judith Butler, who suggests that gender is not fixed, as it is created through iterative processes, and can therefore be subverted from within. In all these writings, although there are claims that change and subversion are possible within the practices of everyday life which are still regarded as highly normative and restrictive, excluding those who don't fit within the norms. All these writings are in stark contrast to the apprehension of the ordinary in our ethnography of blue jeans. We have not regarded the ordinary as either romantic or exclusionary. If anything, our ordinary allows people to live what Butler (1999) calls a livable life. If there is a struggle, it is for the ordinary as a realm that allows people to escape from issues of exclusion or valorization and settle instead into a state of relaxed neutrality.

WHAT IS THE ORDINARY AND WHY DOES IT MATTER?

While Raymond Williams may have helped bolster a tendency toward a romanticizing of ordinary and popular culture, he was certainly instrumental in opening up the study of the ordinary through his central assertion that culture is ordinary. Previously culture tended to be equated narrowly with high culture. However, while much of his essay "Culture Is Ordinary" (1958) involves an exploration of what we mean by the term *culture,* there is no equivalent exploration of *ordinary.* Rather, this is merely implied in terms such as "ordinary people" and "the culture within which he grew up." It is expressed in Williams's discussion of education in particular, as where he states that "learning is ordinary" and that when younger, people learned "where we could" (1958, 93). The contrast is with his subsequent studies at Cambridge, where he encountered "culture, not in any sense I know, but in a special sense: the outward and emphatically visible sign of a special kind of people, cultivated people'"(1958, 93) This is separated from "ordinary people and ordinary work" (1958, 94). Williams's intention clearly is to rescue *culture* from being merely the designation of high culture, insisting that the ordinary be accepted as equally integral to culture. But merely championing the ordinary in this manner may have resulted in the tendency toward romanticization that was alluded to previously. What Williams doesn't really attempt is a fuller designation or exploration of the ordinary in its own right.

Two more recent research projects—Savage, Bagnall, and Longhurst's work (2001a, 2001b) and Gronow and Warde's book *Ordinary Consumption* (2001)—represent a rather more explicit consideration of the ordinary, particularly with its relation to social class. Savage, Bagnall, and Longhurst explore how people use the word *ordinary* to describe themselves. In their research into the middle classes and radio listening, they conclude that a desire to "appear ordinary" is key to understanding the rejection or adoption of a class identity (2001a, 140; see also 2001b). They argue that "ordinariness as a discourse allows people to retreat from social fixing" (2001a, 140)—that is, a person is not reducible to a category of identity. It is of particular significance that they are talking about a discourse, that is, how people verbalize and explain themselves and their class identity. *Ordinary* is not used solely by the working class to define themselves as the common man, as implied by Williams, but rather has quite a fluid presence, available to a wide range of people. This is confirmed by our understanding of the ordinary in our own research on denim. There is no fixed idea or ideal of what an ordinary person is, but it is clearly a designation that matters to many people, and it needs to be appreciated and understood in these terms.

Gronow and Warde's work lies close to the trajectory of studies established by Williams in that they too consider the ordinary in order to explicitly challenge the dominance in studies of consumption of both high culture and symbolic or unusual consumption. With Williams, they insist upon ordinary consumption as what most people do most of the time, but unlike Williams, Gronow and Warde develop a more explicit focus upon the ordinary. In their account, ordinary consumption refers to "those items and practices which are neither highly visible nor in any way special and which often stand in a subsidiary relation to some other primary or more conscious activity" (2001, 4)—for example, the consumption of basic utilities such as gasoline, electricity, and water. Such activities are "mostly taken entirely for granted and without symbolic communicative potential" (2001, 5). They advocate a turn toward the less visible, which has no grounds for being regarded as special and is thereby taken for granted. But they tend to see clothing as an example of more evident symbolic consumption, and thereby fail to see how a garment such as blue jeans can in fact exemplify these very qualities of the taken-for-granted.

As it happens, our study veers away from a focus upon the ordinary as being significant primarily in terms of discussions of class and consumption. We reflect the circumstances of the North London streets in which we worked, where the more evident concern was with immigration and ethnicity. This brings us closer to Gail Lewis (2007) on the "*ordinariness* of racialising culture" (2007, 873) and a consideration of how debates over multiculturalism intersect in the "crucible of the ordinary" (2007, 868). Our ethnography suggests that this is a point of particular significance within contemporary London. Blue jeans, which signify neither a given place of origin nor a particular host society, help migrants negotiate on a daily level the degree to which they may either choose to dress "differently" for a particular occasion or otherwise just get on with their lives. Blue jeans provide a state in which they simply don't have to bother with issues of whether they should assimilate to any norms of the host culture. This seems consistent with a key argument in Lewis that cultural formations are formed by everyone and are not merely an ideological rendition of the dominant or host society.

Jeans provide a medium by which people can sidestep questions of dominance or exclusion, though obviously only inasmuch as these are facets of clothing and appearance.

While all these approaches accord some centrality to the ordinary, they remain embedded in other issues such as class and ethnicity. By contrast, Sandywell attempts to explore and define what ordinariness is in itself. He argues that it has garnered a series of associations by being characterized within different theoretical traditions. The ordinary "implicates a cluster of significations indexing the habitual, customary, regular, usual or normal," and it contrasts with the "*exceptional* or *unusual*" (2004, 162), which tend to be more highly valued since they are rare. Within theoretical discussion, the ordinary, often equated with the popular and everyday, is presumed to be repetitive and ahistorical, though for Sandywell these qualities and the degree to which the ordinary is taken for granted are artifacts of its treatment in theory rather than actual attributes of ordinariness. By contrast, our research suggests that the taken-for-granted nature of denim is central to how we understand the ordinary and that it resonates with our understanding of practice and material culture.

There is some overlap in how anthropology treats the relationship between the ordinary and the normative (as discussed in the previous chapter) and how it is treated within sociology, as exemplified by Goffman's work on stigma. This is one of the texts in which the centrality of the ordinary to sociology is made most apparent. A sense of the ordinary is central to how people establish a norm for a group or a category, whether this is social class, occupation, or what is regarded as a "type" of person. Goffman argues that such categorization is central to interaction, especially in the context of strangers. "Society establishes the means of categorizing persons and the complement of attributes felt to be ordinary and natural for members of each of these categories" (1990, 11). When we initially encounter someone, "first appearances are likely to enable us to anticipate his category and attributes," that is, a person's social identity (1990, 12). Much of the time this is routinized and not given particular or explicit thought. An assumption that this is merely ordinary seems central to this process and thus fundamental to social interaction more generally.

Denim, however, occupies a peculiar position in relation to these ideas, inasmuch as ordinary jeans are what people wear when they wish to avoid being categorized. The sense of being a "type" of person is retained where jeans remain semiotic, as with particular categories of jeans such as those that are more "special" or for "going out," or through combination with other clothing in the wardrobe. Yet for the most part, denim as an expression of the ordinary is precisely what allows people to elude categorization or becoming subject to others' assumptions about what kind of person they are. Wearing jeans does not create a normative category of the ordinary that leads to the stigmatization of those who fail to wear jeans, and therefore it does not follow Goffman's analysis.

In Gronow and Warde's work a central role is granted to habits and routine that are regarded as central to understanding "ordinary" consumption, much of which must be routine and habitual. One of their arguments as to why the ordinary has been neglected is because the concern to understand and appreciate the importance of the routine and the habitual disappeared from social theory after the initial work on this topic by Weber and Durkheim. Drawing from Campbell's more recent discussion, they argue that we need to focus more on these issues. Even if apparently the world is more detraditionalized (and we have more "choice" in, for example, fashion), this does not necessarily mean that we have become reflexive. Action may rest just as much on habit, which follows from what Gronow and Warde describe as "social inertia" (2001, 227–28).

This observation gets to the crux of why the ordinary matters. If this is what most people do most of the time, then it ought to have a central place in sociology. What our research on denim adds to this is that the ordinary is not a state that people necessarily feel restricted by, and it is therefore quite distinct from the norms discussed in, for example, Butler's work. In fact, Butler's (1999) notion of a livable life is precisely what the people in our ethnography are striving toward, and this is achieved for them, in some part, through wearing jeans. Clothing is not necessarily a symbolic domain in which people continually want to invest time and thought. Jeans allow them to shed the burden both of creating identity for themselves and of being identified and potentially stigmatized by others. It seems that, at least some of the time, people wish to be simply ordinary.

ORDINARINESS AND PRACTICAL CONSCIOUSNESS

So far we have reviewed sociological discussions of the nature of the ordinary, why it matters, and why we need to study it. In this section we focus more on the ordinary as something embedded in everyday routine and practical actions rather than made explicit. Even in our own field-work we did not come to our emphasis on the concept of ordinary because this was a term people used regularly in accounts of their jeans wearing. The term *comfortable* (discussed in chapter 4) was far more important. This is in contrast with the experience of Savage, Bagnall, and Longhurst (2001a, 2001b). While they had not anticipated that the ordinary was going to be a key finding of their research, it was precisely the recurrent use of the word *ordinary* that prompted their realization of its importance and their subsequent analysis of how people used it in their accounts. But then their concern was with issues of class, and it is in this area that the ordinary does seem to have particular symbolic resonance, as argued in academic terms by figures such as Williams.

In our denim research something rather different is going on, as in general we found that the relationship people have to their clothing practices is something they struggle to verbalize. So although we started our work by taking people's life histories in relation to jeans and then interviewing them about their wider relationship to jeans, this was always complemented by direct observation. Sometimes we photographed the jeans they possessed or were wearing; sometimes we took notes of our encounters with people on the streets. And sometimes we simply drew inferences from what people did not say, since so much of the practices they described eluded their own explanatory accounts. Or they made verbal claims with regard to areas such as functionality and fit that clearly contradicted or were irrelevant to their actual wearing of jeans.

So while we analyzed what people said about jeans as an artifact in its own right, as with the term *comfortable,* our primary focus comes from the way jeans are embedded in their material practice. In part this corresponds to other writings in sociology, for example by Giddens, who drew partly on Goffman.

A useful way of theorizing and understanding ordinariness as a practice outside of verbal articulation is through Giddens's theory of practical consciousness, which he defines as what people know "tacitly about how to 'go on' in the contexts of social life without being able to give them direct discursive expression" (1986, xxiii). Of central importance to his argument is that idea that even if this is tacit and part of routine practice, it is still in some sense reflexive. A key issue raised by reading Giddens involves his choice of the words *consciousness* and *knowledge.* As we made clear in previous chapters, with respect to their jeans people often seemed to know very little at all. They had often forgotten (if they ever knew) what brand of jeans they were wearing, were not always sure where they had originally purchased them, and on many occasions had no ready account of why they were wearing either these jeans or jeans at all. Obviously our discussion is primarily based on what we did manage to elicit, but many of these people were quite unlikely to have had such discussions other than because of our prompting. For his part, Giddens identifies three kinds of consciousness: the relatively un-reflexive, the reflexive monitoring of conduct, and the deliberation im-plied when we speak of someone "consciously" doing something. It is the second of these that correlates to practical consciousness, which is defined in contrast to "discursive consciousness," which is defined as "being able to put things into words" (Giddens 1986, 45). Put in such terms, it could be said that even when the people we worked with lacked discursive consciousness—that is, they could not put things into words—embedded in the everyday wearing of jeans might still be the knowledge and reflexive awareness that allow them to become ordinary. "Practical consciousness consists of knowing the rules and the tactics whereby daily social life is constituted and reconstituted," writes Giddens (1986, 90). There is a danger of tautology here, in that people may be said to have practical consciousness because they wear jeans, but also to wear jeans in the light of such practical consciousness. On the other hand, this can remain consistent with the idea (discussed in the last chapter) that wearing jeans need not be normative. People are necessarily aware that wearing jeans is a common practice, and they experience a sense of relax-ation when jeans obviate the pressures of choice. This need not pre-sume a relationship to the normative, where they feel obliged or pressured to wear jeans as a moral act. Rather, the point that Giddens is making may be subsumed within the observations that this can become a habitual and routinized action.

From our perspective, the important implication is the respect this grants to knowledge that does not derive from interviews and verbal accounts. It addresses the problem of the degree to which the method-ologies of sociology are overreliant upon language as their source of information. We believe language is better understood as an instrument of legitimation than as a means of explanation. People seem content as long as they can give some kind of "commonsense" account for why they are wearing jeans. If anything, it is these explanations and rational-izations that are normative, in the sense that people may be aware that this is what others expect them to say. But this may have little to do with the routinized and material relationships people have to their jeans. The evidence for this is that people mainly discuss in detail the jeans that we have termed semiotic, those that are special in some way or other. Largely disregarded are those jeans that best express the ordinary in having no particular features upon which people would naturally discourse. We find that people come to such routines, and experience their consequences, more through practice than through discussion. This would not only support Giddens's arguments about practical consciousness but also perhaps go further toward a perspective that Giddens to some degree wished to refute: the sense of practical philosophy associated with the structuralism of Lévi-Strauss, in which mythic and other senses of the world pass across societies and regions according to a higher order and pattern that need never register in consciousness. In reflecting upon the evidence of chapter 5, in which we found that certain principles and ideals such as egalitarianism seem to be fostered by jeans as an aggregate practice rather than as the intention of the individual wearer, we seem to be approaching that more structuralist understanding of how ideas and ideals spread across societies.

ROUTINES

Implicit both in Giddens's discussion and also in Goffman's earlier work on social interaction is people's reliance upon routine. Goffman argues that people are not told the rules of behavior but learn these through practice, observation, and interaction. Giddens believes that practical consciousness is central to everyday life and that this is underpinned by routine. "Ordinary day-to-day life—in greater or less degree according to context and the vagaries of individual personality—involves an *ontological security* expressing an *autonomy of bodily control* within *predictable routines*" (1986, 50). All of this would be equally true of the concept of habitus as used by Bourdieu (1977). In some ways Bourdieu takes us still further along this route, inasmuch as he sees routine practical action as fundamental to the very act of socialization by which people come to be representative of the society in which they are born, but also because in his case much more emphasis is given to the ways in which material objects are ordered and relate to each other to produce meanings and the way material culture itself objectifies these routines, which we follow every time we engage with these objects—for example, the way we use a knife and fork, or the way we walk through a house. The term *habitus* could hardly be a clearer indication of this grounding in routine.

In the work of Bourdieu, routines are not just important in socialization. Habitus becomes the foundation for subsequent practice in a manner that is creative and dynamic rather than mere replication of precedent. This is one of the starting points for the most recent attempt to engage in an explicit understanding of routine by sociologists (and in this case also anthropologists). The collection edited by Shove, Trentmann, and Wilk (2009) challenges many of the previous assumptions that have been made about routine, including the correlation between routine and regularity that was countered by Bourdieu (1977). Trentmann (2009, 8) argues that routine is a result of "repair work" and not mindless repetition. Routine should not be seen in opposition to the seemingly more dynamic instances of rupture; rather, the two are part of the same phenomenon. Slater (2009) challenges traditions found from Marx to the Frankfurt School, which tend to view routines as nonreflexive practices that alienate individuals from who they "really" are. This is not merely the purview of writers in the Marxist tradition, as Weber and Durkheim also regard routine as unreflexive and characteristic of the nonmodern. Wilk (2009) goes on to suggest that a myth of modernization is that people would be freed from routines. Lefebvre in *Rhythmanalysis* (2004) argued that routines are what discipline people, and liberty is an absence of routine; this is tied to the critique of capitalism and its spawn, consumption, where the very abundance of consumer goods and the subservience of our actions to such goods is regarded as enslaving. There is some opposition to such unremittingly negative apprehensions of routine in the work of de Certeau (1984), who examines the creativity in consumption in everyday life. But neither side of such debates seems to approach the kind of situation we have uncovered with regard to denim. We believe it is precisely the routine relationship to jeans as ordinary that is experienced as a form of liberation from the oppressive burdens of identity. Closer to the mark is Wilk (2009), who problematizes the two competing views of modernity that see it as either freeing people from routine or imposing on them the drudgery of routine. Wilk recognizes that habits cannot be assumed to be a tool of restraint; rather, they can be liberating. Much as with the term *ordinary*, one problem is the degree to which the very semantics of the term *routine* have become embedded in various dualisms in which it may be opposed to, for example, choice or spontaneity. As Slater (2009) notes, *routine* tends to encode a moral frame and judgment.

Shove, Trentmann, and Wilk (2009) highlight three key elements that are useful in developing these links between the ordinary and the routine. The first is the diversity of routines. Some but not others may be taken for granted. There are those that "make life possible, and those which make living miserable" (Wilk 2009, 144). Second, Wilk suggests that it is important to adopt a phenomenological approach in order to see how routines are subjectively experienced. Even a seemingly mundane routine can appear different when it is experienced by a person as a time to think or to free the mind. Toward this end Wilk examines the internalization of routine. Sometimes we engage in what he calls "cultivation" (2009, 149), an adaptation of routine that involves a degree of deliberation and reflection; at other times we allow routine to sink back into habit through what he calls "naturalization" (2009, 150). He suggests that much of the time we would prefer the latter, since the former can be exhausting. But we are highly sensitive to any offense we give to others, and even being noticed can drive routine back into consciousness. Our data on jeans accord with this observation. The third element derives from observations by Shove (Shove, Trentmann, and Wilk 2009; Shove 2003) in which she shows how routines are embedded in all aspects of material culture, such as washing machines and thermostats, as well as in social codes. As Shove and Southerton show (2000), a process of normalization parallel to Wilk's model of naturalization may develop in relation to an object such as a freezer and its wider linkages— for example, the use of microwave ovens and the purchase of certain kinds of food from the supermarket.

In our data on jeans we can see much of the diversity reflected in these three perspectives. People may feel liberated from choice, but at a certain stage in their lives they may also feel they have fallen into a rut. They may feel they organize order their wardrobe or that they are allowing the wardrobe to organize them. Sometimes they want and need the kind of routine and sense of the ordinary represented by jeans, and at other times they strive to be eccentric individuals full of spontaneity and the unexpected.

ORDINARINESS AND ROUTINES

This discussion of routine is fundamental to our understanding of the ordinary as an aspect of practice and material culture. Ordinary is something people do, rather than something they strive to be. But in this final section we want to return to the ordinary itself. We noted earlier that there seems to be a discrepancy between our arguments and those of Goffman in *Stigma* (1990), where he argues that the ordinary allows people to categorize others. In Goffman's sense, the ordinary can be part of the process of "profiling" (1990, 68): we develop a sense of what is ordinary for a particular type of person, from which we derive expectations about someone's conduct and character. For example, people who dress in a particular style are often expected to behave in a certain way—as when clothing is designated as marking a particular subculture.

But in our study of denim in these streets we find something entirely different. The very point of blue jeans as the art of the ordinary is that they skip away from any such designations and presumptions. Far from being exclusive and designating who does and does not belong to a certain group, denim seems to equate the ordinary with inclusivity: in this post-semiotic era, absolutely anyone and everyone can and does wear denim. This mirrors the comment by Savage, Bagnall, and Longhurst that "this new type of ordinary 'community' is inclusive in that it incorporates those from groups with previously diverse tastes and backgrounds." In their work, as well as in ours, the ordinary is about inclusion rather than exclusion (Savage, Bagnall, and Longhurst 2001a, 143).

Yet the mechanism by which this power of inclusion works is not so different from stigma as it is discussed by Goffman. Goffman pays great attention not just to what people say but to the way the body (and by inference clothing) acts as a form of "conventionalised discourse"—that is, it may convey certain attributes expected of a person in a particular category. People attempt to fit in and act as those of this particular category are expected to act. This clearly pertains to the question of visibility (Goffman 1990, 64). Goffman argues that visibility is different from "known-about-ness" (65), which is based on wider and deeper prior knowledge of a person. It is also different from "obtrusiveness" (66), which is when particular traits "loom large" in a social situation (125). He suggests that people adopt strategies to avoid being made the center of attention. Goffman discusses this in relationship to stigma and those who stand out, by which he means people who possess "a trait that can obtrude itself upon attention . . . a stigma, an undesired differentness from what we had anticipated" (15). The point applies equally well to the way denim helps people not to stand out or draw attention to themselves, and more generally to avoid being categorized with respect to age, gender, ethnicity, and other such attributes.

Understanding how routines come to be and how they fade away, the role of internalized expectations, and the externalized powers of material culture all help us in our appreciation of how the ordinary

works as an often taken-for-granted aspect of everyday life and practice. But this is not just a matter of theory. In chapter 5 we were concerned with issues that pertain to the fundamental relationship between
immigrants and their host society, thus coming closer to Goffman's discussion of stigma. Our evidence suggests that for all the attention paid
to issues of integration, multiculturalism, and the cosmopolitan in both
social science and politics, the humble unobserved work of the routinized material culture that we call ordinary blue jeans may be just as effective as any government policy or ideology in actually creating a context in which host and migrant can come to terms with each other and
feel a genuine sense of commonality that no longer involves any issue of
superiority, discrimination, and above all stigma. But just because this
aspect of blue jeans ties in with something conventionally recognized as
important to politics does not mean that the other ways jeans matter to
people—for example, in terms of how teenagers respond to parents, the
avoidance of embarrassments at parties, and how people try to escape
the stress of work when they are at home—are not important.

CONCLUSION

This book is about blue jeans as the art of ordinary, but it is also an
example of contemporary material culture studies (Miller 2010). A critical claim of such studies is that they bring into direct juxtaposition the
intensity of the ethnographic encounter and the abstractions of theoretical debates. That is why the early chapters of this volume are largely
descriptive, showing how people relate to denim in terms of their personal history, their social relationships, and the world of shopping and
brands. The middle section of this book is more analytical, trying to
tease apart what is at stake in the use of terms such as *comfortable* and
finding a significance to denim in areas such as migration and the post-
semiotic that might not have been intuitively obvious prior to such
analysis. Finally the book engages directly with theory in anthropology
and sociology to show how these are challenged by our findings, using
the specific lens provided by the concept of the ordinary.

In traveling such a distance, from the parochialism of three streets in
one part of London to a radical departure from the way contemporary
society has been theorized, we have ignored or skimmed over many
questions of context and generalization. This book has had very little
to say about the history of jeans, their production, or marketing, as we
realized that these topics would be better covered by specialists in those

areas. This is why we created the Global Denim Project (www.ucl.ac.uk/global-denim-project). The Global Denim Project is an unusual beast in that it is based on a kind of open-source model, with academics contributing simply out of their interest in so doing. Jeans have an extraordinarily interesting history, one rather more complex than its popular retelling (see especially Comstock 2011). And anthropologists routinely work in areas of the world to which much of jeans production has been subcontracted, such as the Philippines. Our colleagues in this project have tried to convey the difficult conditions of those who try to sell jeans in markets in Brazil (Pinheiro 2011) or work in export-processing zones in Egypt (Chakravarti 2011). We have written elsewhere of the ironies by which workers in Mexico may suffer illness because of chemicals used in trying to fake the "life" of blue jeans (e.g., Miller 2009a; for a discussion outside of our project, see Snyder 2008). We would also like to undertake further projects on the rise of "ethical denim" and on issues of size and fit.

But the contents of this volume were not determined by our interests. We tried to suppress these in favor of listening to and learning from the people that we studied. The informants we worked with showed little interest in who made their jeans or where the jeans came from. If these topics had been more important to them, we would have discussed them further. Even the main theoretical agenda we brought to the topic, that of anxiety, is barely present. What this book contains instead is a reflection of what seemed to matter to our informants. Because this is a material culture study, we did not rely only what they said; our focus emerged just as much from our observation of what they did and what they wore. So there is a chapter on the meanings of the term *comfortable* because it was the single most common term of legitimation used, and there is a chapter on immigration simply because so many of our informants came from abroad and we could discern a significance in jeans that these people might not have drawn attention to.

Blue jeans may be ubiquitous, but the reasons people wear them are not. In the wider context of the Global Denim Project, the limits to generalization from this particular case study are clear. Indeed, our informants noted that the meaning of their jeans seemed very different when they returned to their countries of origin. In almost every other part of the world jeans remain deeply semiotic, with specific local implications. As we have noted several times, it is no coincidence that the emphasis upon the ordinary emerges from a study of London, since London as "nowhere in particular" is at the vanguard of ordinariness as the rejection of other kinds of identity. We are therefore circumspect in our conclusions. We do not presume that the ordinary would be as important in any other region as it is in London, or that the ordinary in London is necessarily some vanguard state that will become more general in the future. Nor can we tell how many other aspects of material culture, whether clothing-related or in other domains, would have exemplified these same points. So we have limited our generalization in this volume to philosophical abstractions, rather than making claims about other objects or other places. But the millions of blue jeans wearers in London are quite sufficient to demonstrate that the claims made in this volume pertain to an extraordinary diversity of people. In our mind, that fully justifies the discussion in the last two chapters of the challenges these claims represent to established social science theory. We look forward to future comparative studies that will provide the scholarly foundations to any further discussion of such generalizations. For example, one colleague recently suggested that the ideas discussed here may prove fertile for examining the ubiquity of rice and beans in Latin America and the Caribbean (Richard Wilk, pers. comm.).

This volume is also intended to add to the corpus of contemporary material culture studies. The aim of such studies is ultimately the rebuilding of our general understanding of humanity through our engagement with its particularity. Material culture studies go beyond the interview and the researchers' understanding of what people say to include the patient observation of what they do—their routines, their practices. Attention to these details is our vehicle for a deep immersion in the experiential sense of denim as something close to the body and a solution to the core anxieties people have over how to appear to the world. But from ethnography we move upward to an analysis of comfort and the post-semiotic and thence to theories of routine and the ordinary. We see how the process of naturalization may help explain both why blue jeans evade the consciousness of the people who wear them and why academics fail to study jeans.

But the benefit of this approach emerges only with the inclusion of both of these discussions in the same volume. Descriptions of jeans wearing alone could have been merely parochial and of limited interest. Similarly, discussion of esoteric social science theory can equally be parochial and of limited interest. What we find exciting is the challenge faced by grounding those theoretical issues in something as mundane as denim and in making the argument that our findings about blue jeans can overthrow anthropological theory's reliance upon the normative.

So this is also a book about the ladder of inference and how material culture studies can help us climb up and down between more abstract and more concrete encounters with cultural life.

When we first started our encounter with blue jeans, we realized that they are a quintessential example of the blindingly obvious—something that has become so ubiquitous and apparently self-evident that it can be hard to see it at all. Despite our relentless studying and writing, we can still fail to even notice, let alone account for, some of the most basic activities of our everyday lives. It is worth noting that in the huge academic literature dedicated to the study of clothing and fashion, there is virtually no mention of denim or blue jeans (see, for example, the journal *Fashion Theory*). We believe that most of what we have written about denim in this book can make the claim of original insight, rather than being a relatively pointless academic recitation of something that most people feel they already knew anyway.

We also hope this helps to vindicate another aspect of material culture studies, which is that in general we do not work from hypotheses or theory but allow the salient features of the study to emerge from the engagement of fieldwork. We remain open to the possibility that the most important results of research are those that we were unaware of prior to commencement of the study. This is entirely antithetical to the culture of grant proposals, for example, which these days tends to insist upon an outline of likely conclusions even before the research has commenced. By contrast, our criteria for the choice of a research subject are twofold: first, that we are researching a topic precisely because we have no clear explanation for it, and second, we study a practice because its sheer scale and extent are themselves the evidence for the likely importance of that practice. The aim of material culture studies is to show how mundane, apparently inconsequential activities constitute the very structure and fabric of our lives, and that they are more powerful and more able to achieve these consequences to the very degree that we fail to perceive them as having any significance at all (Bourdieu 1972; Miller 2010).

Of course, the irony is that if this book accomplishes what it set out to show, it might just disturb a certain kind of equilibrium in which wearing jeans provides a relaxed state outside of self-consciousness and self-interrogation—one of the pleasures of wearing jeans. If this book has made us all rather more aware of such actions and thereby rather less relaxed, we apologize. There is ultimately a radical disjuncture between what we have suggested about blue jeans and the desire of academics to increase the role played by reason and consciousness in life so that we can more effectively make moral choices—a goal influenced by the Enlightenment and by German philosophy. Blue jeans represent something quite remarkably different. They reveal human beings finding a trajectory of moral worth, including a shift toward egalitarianism, that ultimately derives from the aggregate of practice rather than from any conscious decision or reasoning. We have uncovered an apparent tendency for material culture such as blue jeans to achieve certain goals while remaining under the radar of consciousness, so to speak. Hegel would not have approved. But that will just have to remain as the irreconcilable difference between the experience of wearing blue jeans and the experience of writing or reading about them.

Bibliography

Allan, G., and G. Jones. 2003. *Social Relations and the Life Course.* Basingstoke: Palgrave-Macmillan.

Augé, M. 1995. *Non-places: Introduction to an Anthropology of Supermodernity.* London: Verso.

Balfour-Paul, J. 1998. *Indigo.* London: British Museum Press.

Barthes, R. 1967. *The Fashion System.* London: Cape.

Bell, D., and J. Hollows, eds. 2005. *Ordinary Lifestyles: Popular Media, Consumption and Taste.* Maidenhead: Open University Press.

Berger, J. 1972. *Ways of Seeing.* London: Penguin.

Bourdieu, P. 1972. *Esquisse d'une theorie de la pratique, précédé de trois études d'ethnologie kabyle.* Geneva: Droz.

———. 1977. *Outline of a Theory of Practice.* Trans. Richard Nice. Cambridge: Cambridge University Press.

———. 1986. *Distinction: A Social Critique of the Judgment of Taste.* Trans. Richard Nice. London: Routledge.

Brown, M. F. 1996. "On Resisting Resistance." *American Anthropologist* 98, no. 4: 729–49.

Burikova, Z. and Miller, D. 2010. *Au Pair.* London: Polity.

Butler, J. 1999. *Gender Trouble: Feminism and the Subversion of Identity.* London: Routledge.

Chakravarti, L. 2011. "Material Worlds: Denim on the Globalized Shop Floor." In "Unravelling Denim," ed. S. Woodward and D. Miller. Special issue, *Textile: The Journal of Cloth and Culture* 9, no. 1, 62-75.

Chowdhary, U. 2002. "Does Price Reflect Emotional, Structural or Performance Quality?" *International Journal of Consumer Studies* 26, no. 2: 128-33.

Clarke, A. 2000. "'Mother Swapping': The Trafficking of Nearly New Children's Wear." In *Commercial Cultures,* ed. P. Jackson, M. Lowe, D. Miller, and F. Mort. Oxford: Berg.

Clarke, A., and D. Miller. 2002. "Fashion and Anxiety." *Fashion Theory* 6, no. 2: 191–213.

Comstock, S. C. 2011. "The Making of an American Icon: The Transformation of Blue Jeans During the Great Depression." In *Global Denim*, ed. D. Miller and S. Woodward, 23–50. Oxford: Berg.

Connell, R. 2005. *Masculinities*. Cambridge: Polity.

Corrigan, P. 1995. "Gender and the Gift: The Case of the Family Clothing Economy." In *The Politics of Domestic Consumption*, ed. S. Jackson and S. Moores. London: Prentice Hall.

Corsten, M. 1999. "The Time of Generation." *Time and Society* 8: 249–72.

de Certeau, M. 1984. *The Practice of Everyday Life*. Berkeley: University of California Press.

De Grazia, V., and E. Furlough, eds. 1996. *The Sex of Things: Gender and Consumption in Historical Perspective*. Berkeley: University of California Press.

Douglas, M. 1978. *Implicit Meanings: Essays in Anthropology*. London: Routledge.

Durkheim, E. 1976 [1912]. *The Elementary Forms of the Religious Life*. London: Allen and Unwin.

Edwards, T. 2005. *Cultures of Masculinity*. London: Routledge.

Ege, M. 2011. "Picaldi Jeans and the Figuration of Working-Class Male Youth Identities in Berlin: An Ethnographic Account." In *Global Denim*, ed. D. Miller and S. Woodward, 159–80. Oxford: Berg.

Eriksen, T. H. 2001. *Small Places, Large Issues: An Introduction to Social and Cultural Anthropology*. London: Pluto.

Fletcher, K. 2008. *Sustainable Fashion and Textiles*. London: Earthscan.

Fournier, S. 1998. "Consumers and Their Brands: Developing Relationships Theory in Consumer Research." *Journal of Consumer Research* 24: 343–73.

Fox, K. 2005. *Watching the English*. London: Hodder and Stoughton.

Frierson, P. R. 2003. *Freedom and Anthropology in Kant's Moral Philosophy*. Cambridge: Cambridge University Press.

Geertz, C. 2000. *Available Light: Anthropological Reflections on Philosophical Topics*. Princeton: Princeton University Press.

Giddens, A. 1986. *The Constitution of Society: Outline of a Theory of Structuration*. Berkeley: University of California Press.

Gilleard, C., and P. Higgs. 2005. *Contexts of Ageing: Class, Cohort and Community*. Cambridge: Polity.

Gilroy, P. 1987. *There Ain't No Black in the Union Jack: The Cultural Politics of Race and Nation*. London: Hutchinson.

———. 2004. *After Empire: Multiculture or Postcolonial Melancholia*. London: Routledge.

Global Lifestyle Monitor. 2008. *Global Lifestyle Monitor Survey on Denim*. Cotton Council International, Cotton Incorporated, and Synovate. Available at www.cottoninc.com/supplychaininsights/europeanviewsonfiberanddenim/europeanviewsonfiberanddenim.pdf. Accessed June 14, 2010.

Goffman, E. 1975. *Frame Analysis*. Harmondsworth: Penguin.

———. 1990. *Stigma: Notes on the Management of Spoiled Identity*. Harmondsworth: Penguin.

Gombrich, E. 1979. *The Sense of Order*. London: Phaidon.

Gronow, J., and A. Warde, eds. 2001. *Ordinary Consumption*. London: Routledge.

Gullestad, M. 1996. *Everyday Life Philosophers: Modernity, Morality and Autobiography in Norway*. Oslo: Scandinavian University Press.

Hang, K. 2006. *The Denim Bible: Jeans Encyclopaedia II*. Milan: Sportswear International.

Haywood, C., and M. Mac an Ghaill. 2003. *Men and Masculinities: Theory, Research, and Social Practice*. Buckingham: Open University Press.

Hebdige, D. 1979. *Subculture: The Meaning of Style*. London: Routledge.

Hockey, J. 2002. "Interviews as Ethnography? Disembodied Social Interaction in Britain." In *British Subjects*, ed. N. Rapport, 209–22. Oxford: Berg.

Hogbin, I. 1970. *The Island of Menstruating Men: Religion in Wogeo, New Guinea*. Scranton, PA: Chandler.

Hoggart, R. 1969. *The Uses of Literacy*. Harmondsworth: Penguin.

Holland, J., and L. Adkins, eds. 1996. *Sex, Sensibility and the Gendered Body*. Basingstoke: Palgrave Macmillan.

Hollows, J. 2000. *Feminism, Femininity and Popular Culture*. Manchester: Manchester University Press.

Honneth, A. 1995. *The Struggle for Recognition: The Moral Grammar of Social Conflicts*. Trans. Joel Anderson. Cambridge: Polity.

Hoskins, J. 1998. *Biographical Objects: How Things Tell the Stories of People's Lives*. London: Routledge.

Johnston, R., J. Forrest, and M. Poulsen. 2002. "Are There Ethnic Enclaves/ Ghettos in English Cities?" *Urban Studies* 39: 591–618.

Kant, I. 1999 [1781]. *The Critique of Pure Reason*. Cambridge: Cambridge University Press.

———. 2006. *Anthropology from a Pragmatic Point of View*. Ed. R. B. Louden. Cambridge: Cambridge University Press.

Keane, W. 2005. "Signs Are Not the Garb of Meaning: On the Social Analysis of Material Things." In *Materiality*, ed. D. Miller, 182–205. Durham: Duke University Press.

Keet, P. 2011. "Making New Vintage Jeans in Japan: Relocating Authenticity." In "Unravelling Denim," ed. S. Woodward and D. Miller. Special issue, *Textile: The Journal of Cloth and Culture* 9, no. 1, 44-61.

Koda, H., and A. Bolton. 2005. *Chanel*. New York: Metropolitan Museum of Art.

Lawler, S. 2002. "Narrative in Social Research." In *Qualitative Research in Action*, ed. T. May, 242–58. London: Sage.

Lefebvre, H. 2004. *Rhythmanalysis: Space, Time and Everyday Life*. New York: Continuum.

———. 1991. *Critique of Everyday Life*. London: Verso.

Lewis, G. 2007. "Racialising Culture Is Ordinary." *Cultural Studies* 21, no. 6, 111-29.

Lofgren, O. 1994. "Consuming Interests." In *Consumption and Identity*, ed. J. Friedman. Chur, Switzerland: Harwood Academic.

Lury, C. 1996. *Consumer Culture*. Cambridge: Polity.

Malaby, T. M. 2009. *Making Virtual Worlds: Linden Lab and Second Life.* Ithaca, NY: Cornell University Press.

Mann, C. 1996. "Girl's Own Story: The Search for a Sexual Identity in Times of Family Change." In *Sex, Sensibility and the Gendered Body,* ed. J. Holland and L. Adkins. Basingstoke: Palgrave Macmillan.

McCracken, G. 1989. "'Homeyness': A Cultural Account of One Constellation of Consumer Goods and Meanings." In *Interpretive Consumer Research,* ed. E. Hirschman. Provo, UT: Association for Consumer Research.

McDonald, T. 2011. "'Cowboy Cloth' and Kinship: The Closeness of Denim Consumptions in a South-west Chinese City." In "Unravelling Denim," ed. S. Woodward and D. Miller. Special issue, *Textile: The Journal of Cloth and Culture* 9, no. 1, 76-89.

Mead, G. H. 1913. "The Social Self." *Journal of Philosophy, Psychology, and Scientific Methods* 10: 374–80.

Merry, S. E. 2001. "Changing Rights, Changing Culture." In *Culture and Rights: Anthropological Perspectives,* ed. J. K. Cowan, M.-B. Dembour, and R. A. Wilson, 31–55. Cambridge: Cambridge University Press.

Miller, D. 1987. *Material Culture and Mass Consumption.* Oxford: Blackwell.

———. 1997. "How Infants Grow Mothers in North London." *Theory, Culture and Society* 14, no. 4: 67–88.

———. 1998. *A Theory of Shopping.* Cambridge: Polity Press.

———, ed. 2005. *Materiality.* Durham, NC: Duke University Press.

———. 2008. *The Comfort of Things.* Cambridge: Polity Press.

———. 2009a. "Buying Time." In *Time, Consumption and Everyday Life,* ed. E. Shove, F. Trentmann, and R. Wilk, 157–70. Oxford: Berg.

———, ed. 2009b. *Anthropology and the Individual.* Oxford: Berg.

———. 2010. *Stuff.* Cambridge: Polity.

———. 2011. "The Limits of Jeans in Kannur," In *Global Denim,* ed. D. Miller and S. Woodward, 23–50. Oxford: Berg.

Miller, D., and S. Woodward. 2007. "A Manifesto for the Study of Denim." *Social Anthropology* 15, no. 3: 335–51.

———, eds. 2011. *Global Denim.* Oxford: Berg.

Mintel Market Research. 2007. "Jeans—April 2007." London: Mintel International Group.

Mizrahi, M. 2011. "'Brazilian Jeans': Materiality, Body and Seduction at Rio de Janeiro's Funk Ball." In *Global Denim,* ed. D. Miller and S. Woodward, 103–26. Oxford: Berg.

Mort, F. 1996. *Cultures of Consumption.* London: Routledge.

Mulvey, L. 1975. "Visual Pleasure and Narrative Cinema." *Screen* 16, no. 3: 6–18.

Olesen, B. 2011. "How Blue Jeans Went Green: The Materiality of an American Icon." In *Global Denim,* ed. D. Miller and S. Woodward, 69–86. Oxford: Berg.

Olwig. K. F. 1993. *Global Culture, Island Identity: Continuity and Change in the Afro-Caribbean Community of Nevis.* Chur, Switzerland: Harwood.

Ortner, S. B. 1984. "Theory in Anthropology Since the Sixties." *Comparative Studies in Society and History* 26, no. 1: 126–66.

Parekh, B. C. 2000. *Rethinking Multiculturalism: Cultural Diversity and Political Theory.* London: Palgrave Macmillan.

Peach, C. 1996. "Does Britain Have Ghettos?" *Transactions of the Institute of British Geographers,* n.s., 21, 1: 216–35.

Pinheiro, R. 2011. "The Jeans That Don't Fit: Marketing Cheap Jeans in Brazil." In *Global Denim,* ed. D. Miller and S. Woodward, 181–96. Oxford: Berg.

Pink, S. 2009. *Doing Sensory Ethnography.* London: Sage.

Rabinow, P. 1999. *French DNA: Trouble in Purgatory.* Chicago: University of Chicago Press.

Reinach, S. 2005. "China and Italy: Fast Fashion Versus Prêt à Porter: Towards a New Culture of Fashion." *Fashion Theory* 9, no. 1: 43–56.

Ricoeur, P. 1987. *Time and Narrative III.* Chicago: University of Chicago Press.

Riello, G., and P. Parthasarathi, eds. 2009. *The Spinning World: A Global History of Cotton Textiles, 1200–1850.* Pasold Studies in Textile History. Oxford: Oxford University Press.

Rouse, J. 2007a. "Practice Theory." In *Philosophy of Anthropology and Sociology,* ed. S. P. Turner and M. W. Risjord, 639–81. Amsterdam: Elsevier.

———. 2007b. "Social Practices and Normativity." *Philosophy of the Social Sciences* 37, no. 1: 1–11.

Sahlins, M. 1976. *Culture and Practical Reason.* Chicago: University of Chicago Press.

Sandywell, B. 2004. "The Myth of Everyday Life: Toward a Heterology of the Ordinary." *Cultural Studies* 18, nos. 2/3: 160–80.

Sartre, J.-P. 1969. *Being and Nothingness: An Essay on Phenomenological Ontology.* London: Routledge.

Sassatelli, R. 2011. "Indigo Bodies: Fashion, Mirror Work and Sexual Identity in Milan." In *Global Denim,* ed. D. Miller and S. Woodward, 127–44. Oxford: Berg.

Savage, M., G. Bagnall, and B. Longhurst. 2001a. "Ordinary Consumption and Personal Identity." In *Ordinary Consumption,* ed. J. Gronow and A. Warde. London: Routledge.

———. 2001b. "Ordinary, Ambivalent and Defensive: Class Identities in the Northwest of England." *Sociology* 35: 875.

Scheper-Hughes, N. 1995. "The Primacy of the Ethical: Propositions for a Militant Anthropology." *Current Anthropology* 36, no. 3: 409–20.

Schrempp, G. 1989. "Aristotle's Other Self." In *Romantic Motives: Essays on Anthropological Sensibility,* ed. G. W. Stocking Jr., 10–43. Madison: University of Wisconsin Press.

Shove, E. 2003. *Comfort, Cleanliness and Convenience.* Oxford: Berg.

Shove, E and Southerton, D., 2000. "Defrosting the Freezer: From Novelty to Convenience: A Story of Normalization." *Journal of Material Culture* 5, no. 2, 301-19.

Shove, E., F. Trentmann, and R. Wilk, eds. 2009. *Time, Consumption and Everyday Life.* Oxford: Berg.

Simmel, G. 1957. "Fashion." *American Journal of Sociology* 62: 541–58.

Simpson, L. 2007. "Ghettos of the Mind: The Empirical Behaviour of Indices of Segregation and Diversity." *Journal of the Royal Statistical Society, Series A,* 170: 405–24.

Slater, D. 2009. "The Ethics of Routine: Consciousness, Tedium and Value." In *Time, Consumption and Everyday Life,* ed. E. Shove, F. Trentmann, and R. Wilk. Oxford: Berg.

Snyder, R. L. 2008. *Fugitive Denim.* New York: Norton.

South Carolina Cotton Museum. 2007. *The History of Cotton.* Virginia Beach, VA: Donning.

Sullivan, J. 2006. *Jeans: A Cultural History of an American Icon.* New York: Gotham.

Synovate. 2008. *Fact Global Denim Survey.* Available at www.synovate.com. Accessed June 14, 2010.

Tarhan, M., and M. Sarsiisik. 2009. "Comparison Among Performance Characteristics of Various Denim Fading Processes." *Textile Research Journal* 79, no. 4: 301–9.

Tarlo, E. 2010. *Visably Muslim.* Oxford: Berg.

Taussig, M. 2008. "Redeeming Indigo." *Theory, Culture and Society* 25, no. 3: 1–15.

Taylor, C. 2002. *Multiculturalism and the Politics of Recognition: An Essay.* Princeton Princeton University Press.

Trentmann, F. 2009. "Disruption Is Normal: Blackouts, Breakdowns and the Elasticity of Everyday Life." In *Time, Consumption and Everyday Life,* ed. E. Shove, F. Trentmann, and R. Wilk. Oxford: Berg.

Tungate, M. 2005. *Fashion Brands: Branding Style from Armani to Zara.* London: Kogan Page.

Turner, S. P. 2005. "Normative All the Way Down." *Studies in History and Philosophy of Science, Part A,* 36, no. 2: 419–29.

———. 2007. "Explaining Normativity." *Philosophy of the Social Sciences* 37, no. 1: 57–73.

———. 2010. *Explaining the Normative.* Cambridge: Polity.

Veblen, T. 1899. *Theory of the Leisure Class: An Economic Study of Institutions.* New York: Mentor.

Vinken, B. 2005. *Fashion Zeitgeist.* Oxford: Berg.

Whitehead, S., and F. Barrett. 2001. *The Masculinities Reader.* Cambridge: Polity.

Wilk, R. 1997. "A Critique of Desire: Distaste and Dislike in Consumer Behavior." *Consumption, Markets and Culture* 1, no. 2: 175–96.

———. 2009. "The Edge of Agency: Routines, Habits and Volition." In *Time, Consumption and Everyday Life,* ed. E. Shove, F. Trentmann, and R. Wilk, 143–54. Oxford: Berg.

Wilkinson-Weber, C. 2011. "Diverting Denim: Screening Jeans in Bollywood." In *Global Denim,* ed. D. Miller and S. Woodward, 51–68. Oxford: Berg.

Williams, R. 1958. "Culture Is Ordinary." In R. Williams, *Resources of Hope: Culture, Democracy, Socialism.* London: Verso.

Wilson, E. 1985. *Adorned in Dreams.* London: Routledge.

Woodward, S. 2005. "Looking Good: Feeling Right—Aesthetics of the Self." In *Clothing as Material Culture,* ed. S. Küchler and D. Miller, 21–40. Oxford: Berg.

———. 2007. *Why Women Wear What They Wear.* Oxford: Berg.

———. 2009. "The Myth of Street Style in Fashion Theory." *Journal of Dress, Body and Culture* 13, no. 1: 83–102.

———. 2010. "Unarticulated Narratives of Denim Jeans: The Life Course and Generation." In *The Auto/Biography Yearbook,* ed. A. Sparkes. Southampton: British Sociological Association.

———. 2011. "Jeanealogies: Materiality and the (Im)permanence of Relationships and Intimacy." In *Global Denim,* ed. D. Miller and S. Woodward. Oxford: Berg.

Woodward, S., and D. Miller, eds. 2011. "Unravelling Denim." Special issue, *Textile: The Journal of Cloth and Culture* 9, no. 1.

Young, I. M. 2005. *On Female Body Experience: Throwing Like a Girl and Other Essays.* Oxford: Oxford University Press.

Zurn, C. 2000. "Anthropology and Normativity: A Critique of Axel Honneth's 'Formal Conception of Ethical Life.'" *Philosophy and Social Criticism* 26, no. 1: 115–24.

Index

TEXT
10/13 Sabon

DISPLAY
Sabon

COMPOSITOR
Westchester Book Group

PRINTER AND BINDER
Maple-Vail Book Manufacturing Group